From the Beginning

From the Beginning

A PICTURE HISTORY
OF THE FIRST FOUR DECADES OF
BRANDEIS UNIVERSITY

Editor: Susan Pasternack

Photographers: Ralph Norman · Julian Brown

Photo Archivist: Lisa Webb

Foreword by Paul A. Freund

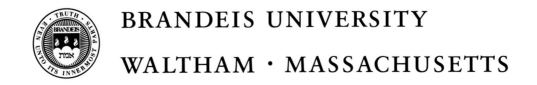

BRANDEIS UNIVERSITY

WALTHAM · MASSACHUSETTS

OPENING ENDLEAVES:
*Panorama of the 1959 commencement
ceremony at Ullman Amphitheatre.*

PAGES II-III:
*Students departing Castle for outing,
ca. 1948.*

PAGES IV-V:
*An early outdoor class led by founding
faculty member Shlomo Marenof,
assistant professor of Near Eastern
languages and civilizations, ca. 1950.*

FRONTISPIECE:
*Students at work in library beneath a
portrait of Justice Brandeis, ca. 1950.
Courtesy* Look *magazine.*

PAGE XII:
*A student trio rehearses on the grounds
near the Slosberg Music Building,
ca. 1960.*

© 1988 by Brandeis University Pictorial
History Project
All rights reserved
Printed in the United States of America

Library of Congress Catalog Card
Number: 88-71191
ISBN 0-9620545-0-X

Brandeis University
Department of Communications and
Public Relations
Sallie K. Riggs, Vice President

Designed by Susan Marsh
Composed by Monotype Composition Co.
Printed by Meriden-Stinehour Press

We gratefully acknowledge the support of Jacob Hiatt in the publication of this pictorial history. In celebrating the first forty years of the University, we also celebrate more than three decades of Jacob Hiatt's dedication to Brandeis. Elected to the Board of Trustees in 1962, and serving as its chairman from 1971 to 1977, Jacob Hiatt has shared his enthusiasm, his energy, his vision, and to echo his honorary degree citation, "his abiding belief in our present and our future."

In thirty years of involvement with Brandeis, Jacob Hiatt has supported a number of University programs, ranging from scholarship aid to annual giving campaigns. In 1961 Brandeis established the Jacob Hiatt Institute in Israel, a traveling university with the State of Israel as its campus. Initially organized for Brandeis students, the Hiatt Institute evolved into a national foreign study program providing educational opportunities for more than 600 students from nearly 150 American colleges and universities. The Hiatt Institute became a model for dozens of other programs of foreign study.

In 1985 Jacob Hiatt endowed the Hiatt Career Development Center at Brandeis offering students skilled professional assistance to enable them to find ways to relate their liberal arts education to future career plans. With services ranging from internship opportunities to computer-assisted guidance, the Hiatt Career Center has become an important campus resource for Brandeis students. In January 1986, in memory of the seven astronauts who died in the explosion of the space shuttle, Jacob Hiatt established the Challenger Memorial Scholarship. The Challenger Scholarship, given in recognition of academic achievement, was endowed to encourage in young Americans the development of qualities exhibited by the crew of the Challenger space shuttle.

Through his many contributions, Jacob Hiatt has continued to show his deep and abiding faith in young people. His vision of education and educational opportunity are exemplified not only by his benevolence to Brandeis, but also by his record of philanthropy in his home city of Worcester.

With thanks, we offer our appreciation to Brandeis trustee and friend, Jacob Hiatt.

CONTENTS

*Portrait of Louis Dembitz Brandeis taken in Boston prior
to his appointment to the United States Supreme Court,
ca. 1915. Courtesy Goodman Engraving Company.*

FOREWORD

"In the Name of Brandeis"

From the beginning, forty years ago, there was general recognition that the greatest asset of Brandeis University, and its greatest challenge, lay in its name. The original Board of Trustees, in its formal invitation to colleges, universities, and learned societies to send delegates to the inaugural ceremonies, made the linkage plain: "We have named the university in honor of the late Justice Louis Dembitz Brandeis, eminent for his contributions to jurisprudence and education and to the welfare of his people. In so honoring him we hope to create an enduring monument to the integrity of his Americanism and to the prophetic quality of his Judaism. Our vision has been charged by the challenge contained in his ideal of a great university. 'It must always be rich in goals and ideals, seemingly attainable but beyond immediate reach. . . . It must become truly a seat of learning where research is pursued, books written, and the creative instinct is aroused, encouraged, and developed in its faculty and students.'"

In concluding his very moving inaugural address, President Sachar echoed these sentiments. He said: "The University begins with immense good will. The name that blesses it is a perpetual challenge. God willing, we shall strive together, trustees, benefactors, faculty, and students, to make it worthy of the name and the challenge."

This spirit of the Founders has been persistent and pervasive through the ensuing years. A monumental sculptured likeness commands the landscape of the campus. How broadly the legacy of the name permeates the life of the institution can be seen in the fact – to descend a little from the sublime – that the athletic teams are not called the Bears or the Blues; they are known as the Judges.

How the Justice would have responded to the creation of this University, or precisely how he would have described its mission, we cannot of course know. He died in November 1941, a few weeks before we entered World War II. But we do know his views on higher education, and on the profession of teaching. When he learned that several more of his former law clerks had become professors, he said proudly, "Now I have a majority." Indeed, he thought of his judicial office as ideally a niche for learning and teaching. "What is so wonderful about deciding cases?" he would reply to friends who rhapsodized over a seat on the Court. I recall the first case on which I worked as his law clerk, where the opinion had gone through perhaps a dozen revisions and was finally, I thought, in untouchable form. "The opinion," he said, "is now persuasive, but what can we do to make it more instructive?" His delivery of opinions from the bench resembled, in its earnestness and intimacy, the discourse of an engaged professor before a small class of students.

We know more particularly his ideas of a university from his letters in the 1920s on the occasion of his donation of large segments of his library to the University of Louisville, in his native city. The brief excerpts quoted earlier in this Foreword are taken from those letters. "To become great, a University must express the people whom

The entrance to Brandeis University with the newly-constructed Slosberg Music Building in view, summer 1957.

it serves, and must express the people and the community at their best." He was addressing what was then a local urban institution; he would have had to envision the community served by Brandeis University as the nation and the world. Size in itself was not an objective; indeed giantism would be a severe handicap in fostering those associations between mentor and learner that are at the heart of true education. He would have deplored the emergence of those huge multiversities, with their tens of thousands of students, which consist of an array of departments and schools loosely connected by underground pipes. Of a college faculty he wrote, "Teachers are largely a meek, downtrodden, unappreciated body of men. To know that others believe in them, consider them capable of high thinking and doing, and are willing to help them out – may enable them to accomplish more than even they think possible." Whether this assessment (made in 1924) would now be regarded by academic administrators as egregiously outdated, I must leave to others to say.

We can be sure that the Justice would have appreciated the values reflected in E.M. Forster's novel, *Howards End,* published prophetically in 1921, where Uncle Ernst, having migrated from Germany to England, is speaking to his German nephew: "It is the vice of a vulgar mind to be thrilled by bigness, to think that a thousand square miles are a thousand times more wonderful than one square mile, and that a million square miles are almost the same as heaven. That is not imagination. No, it kills it. . . . Your Universities? Oh, yes, you have learned men, who collect more facts than do the learned men of England. They collect facts, and facts, and empires of facts. But which of them will rekindle the light within?" One is reminded of the characterization of the Justice by Chief Justice Hughes: "master of both microscope and telescope" – not a bad prescription for a university itself.

A question that must have been faced by the Founders is whether the concept of a Jewish-supported university is not an anachronism, likely to intensify the separatism of Jewish and non-Jewish scholars and spread the blight of discrimination. The answer that Brandeis would have given was foreshadowed by his advice when a similar question was put to him concerning the plans for a Jewish-supported hospital in Boston. If the quality of the institution was kept high, he counseled, Jewish professionals would enjoy greater esteem and admiration, and would be more warmly sought after by their colleagues. It proved to be an accurate diagnosis.

My own feeling of attachment to Brandeis University derives not merely from attachment to its name. An institution, after all, would be a hollow shell without active shapers and guides. As it happens, this institution's first president and indefatigable leader was a boyhood hero of mine. Abram Sachar had a brilliant career at Washington University in St. Louis as an undergraduate and graduate student a decade before I entered as a freshman. He had gone on for postgraduate study at Cambridge University under the renowned historian J.B. Bury, and had become an outstanding scholar and greatly appreciated lecturer at the University of Illinois, as well as a director of the Hillel Foundation. I am not sure whether the term role model had then been invented, but he served as such to those of us who contemplated a life in academia. If Abram Sachar was not the "onelie begetter" of Brandeis University, he was fortunately its shaper and mover and shaker during its crucial formative years. He has been followed in the office by a succession of scholars mindful of the standards he set, and now, reflecting the current of our social and intellectual culture, the presidency is held by — a scientist. Evelyn Handler is happily a scientist with a difference: an empiricist, yes, but a humanist as well, a factfinder with an inner light, a master of both microscope and telescope.

Justice Brandeis's formula for success was fourfold: brains, rectitude, singleness of purpose — and time. Twoscore years are an absurdly short time span for the emergence of a great university. Yet the "seemingly attainable, but beyond immediate reach" has been achieved. The university whose first catalogue listed a faculty of fourteen, including a proctor, an assistant librarian, a visiting lecturer, and one full professor, has become an institution of worldwide distinction and prestige. The story of this dramatic development is documented vividly in this pictorial history.

And what of the next forty years? For answer, I think Justice Brandeis would turn to a favorite line from Goethe: "You must labor to possess that which you have inherited."

PAUL A. FREUND, LL.D. '74

ACKNOWLEDGMENTS

Brandeis University is four decades old, with a history so rich, so varied, and so complex that a single volume can tell but a small part of the story. From more than a quarter of a million photographs in the University collections, we have selected the most telling to give a picture of Brandeis in all its moods and guises. Providing a frame for the photographs are introductions highlighting major events and developments, a colorful context, in a sense, for the vivid images in black and white.

With the assistance and support of the Pictorial History Advisory Committee, it was decided to organize this book developmentally, tracing the major events and decisions crucial to the evolution of the University. Chronologies of events are included insofar as they convey a sense of time and relate to the major themes and developments. *From the Beginning: A Picture History of the First Four Decades of Brandeis University* is not intended to serve as a comprehensive or definitive institutional history. We hope to convey, however, through the power of the photographs, and explanatory captions and text, an image of the extraordinary achievement that is Brandeis University.

The Brandeis pictorial history began with the vision of President Evelyn E. Handler. We have striven to give form and substance to her idea.

This book would not have been possible without the advice, support, encouragement, and discerning eye of Sallie Riggs, Vice President for Communications and Public Relations. Under the auspices of her office, this book became a reality.

I would like to thank our photo archivist Lisa Webb, whose profound appreciation and understanding of the art of photography are reflected in this pictorial history.

I would like to acknowledge and thank the members of the Brandeis Advisory Committee: Chairman Jack Goldstein, Gerald Bernstein, Lawrence Fuchs, Barbara K. Kravitz '57, Trustee Paul Levenson '52, Ricardo Morant, and Phyllis Shapiro, whose reflections brought the history of Brandeis to life, along with remembrances shared by Hannah Abrams, Stuart Altman, Carl Belz, Catherine Butler, Jacques Cohen, Jeff Cohen '64, Saul G. Cohen, John Foti, Frank Gilbert, Faire Goldstein, Allen Grossman, Michael Hammerschmidt '72, John-Edward Hill, Milton Hindus, William Jencks, Shelley Kaplan, Norm Levine, Jack Molloy, Charles Napoli '58, Richard Palais, Abram L. Sachar, and Silvan Schweber.

Thanks to the Brandeis Library staff members who enabled me to use the materials of the Brandeis University Library Special Collections: Ethan Barry, Martha Barry, Victor Berch '66, Charles Cutter, and John Faverman, Ph.D. '87. My gratitude also to current and former members of the staff of the Department of Communications and Public Relations who have watched this entire project unfold and so graciously offered their assistance and support: Sara Barber, Veronica Blacquier, Kimberly Bumstead, Mary Cervantes, Steve Cohen, Charles Dunham, Anita Flanzbaum, Helen Francini, Peggy Hogan, Brian Kologe, David Lennon, Mike McDowell, Esme McTighe, Brenda Marder, Robert Mitchell, Dennis Nealon, Judy Powell, John Rosario, and Laura Wildman. And to the staff of the National Women's Committee and other members of the Brandeis community who have helped in a myriad of ways: Betsy Ball, Diana Beaudoin, Paula Charland '88, Victor Ford, Jack Fracasso, Tanya Gardiner-Scott, Edith Gillette, John Hose, Zina Jordan '61, David Kaplan, Lisa Leary, Carolyn Locke, Nathan Lubofsky '58, Paul Morrison, Mary O'Neill, Cecile Papirno, Sally Phillips, Amy Prussack, Carol Rabinovitz '59, Cynthia Rose, Betsy Rosenberg, Carole Taylor, Thompson Williams, and Judy Zimmerman. Thanks also to Robert P. Fisler. And my special gratitude to Fred Weissman.

The archives of the Brandeis University Libraries Special Collections and the Brandeis University Office of News and Media Relations provided most of the original and secondary source material for this publication, including files of the *Justice*, the *Brandeis Quarterly*, the *Brandeis Reporter*, the *Brandeis Review*, the *Brandeis University Bulletin*, and the *Brandeis University Gazette*, as well as Brandeis University general catalogues and yearbooks, Middlesex University materials, and miscellaneous Brandeis University publications. Additional information was also drawn from: Morris B. Abram, *The Day Is Short* (New York: Harcourt Brace Jovanovich, 1982); David Alexander, "The Brandeis Challenge"; Saul G. Cohen, "Reflections at Retirement" and "Why A Research University"; Bernard Flexner, *Mr. Justice Brandeis and the University of Louisville* (Louisville: University of Louisville, 1938); Israel Goldstein, *Brandeis University: Chapter of Its Founding* (New York: Bloch Publishing, 1951); Clark Kerr, *The Uses of the University* (Cambridge, Mass.: Harvard University Press, 1963); Milton Lomask, *A Minor Miracle: An Informal History of the National Science Foundation* (Washington, D.C.: National Science Foundation, 1976); Louis I. Newman, *A Jewish University in America* (New York: Bloch Publishing, 1923); Gary H. Quehl, "Higher Education and the Public Interest: A Report to the Campus" (Washington, D.C.: Council for Advancement and Support of Education, 1988); and Abram L. Sachar, *A Host at Last* (Boston: Little, Brown and Company, 1976).

Brandeis at forty is testament to the courage, integrity, and vision of its founders and all who have contributed their time, their resources, their energy, and their devotion to this University. It is not possible to recount the names of all those who have nurtured and supported the University throughout its history. We trust that the pages of this book, filled with images of accomplishment and achievement, are a fitting tribute.

We would like to thank the members of the Brandeis University Board of Trustees and the eight Chairmen of the Board, whose unfailing devotion has sustained Brandeis from dream to fulfillment.

SUSAN PASTERNACK

THE FOUNDING

"A Colorful Prologue"

"A commitment to excellence is not that unusual, but an unfaltering, unfailing devotion to its continuation is. Commitment made from the start: acknowledged by all, and adhered to from one generation to the next."

GEORGE ALPERT
Founding Chairman, Brandeis University Board of Trustees

For forty years Brandeis University has held fast to the dream and commitment of its founders to establish a modern university of excellence. Without abandoning those principles that shaped its creation, Brandeis has succeeded in telescoping generations of academic development into four decades.

Founded in 1948, Brandeis University is the realization of a dream, long held and long deferred, the gift of American Jewry to higher education. In 1923 Rabbi Louis I. Newman traced the history of the dream in his volume, *A Jewish University in America*, and concluded, "No one need claim originality for the idea: surely it is big enough and obvious enough to have occurred to many people at various times . . . ."

For nearly three centuries before the founding of Brandeis, the nation's sectarian groups had nurtured institutions of higher learning. Many of America's eminent universities endure as monuments to the inspiration, foresight, and generosity of their denominational forebears.

Brandeis University, however, was nonsectarian from the start. The pledge by the founders to offer opportunities to all was as profound as the commitment to excellence. It was a pledge that would not be compromised by the exigencies of political style or philosophical fashion. The earliest Brandeis documents characterized a university of quality and responsibility, an institution "choosing its faculty on the basis of capacity and creativity and its students by the criteria of academic merit and promise."

The ending of World War II provided the moment for founding the university. Veterans returning from wartime service placed an unprecedented demand on America's educational resources. A generation of young men and women looked to a promising future in a nation at peace. The enactment of the G. I. Bill of Rights ensured educational opportunities for all.

OPPOSITE AND PRECEDING PAGE:
Sculptor Robert Berks directing emplacement of his statue of Justice Brandeis on campus, November 1956. The work was commissioned by Trustee Lawrence Wien as part of the University celebration of the Justice Brandeis Centennial. Berks was later commissioned to create a bust of President Kennedy for the Kennedy Center in Washington.

I

Founding faculty member Dr. Joseph Israel Cheskis, professor of Romance languages and Chairman of the School of Humanities, ca. 1952. As Dean of the College of Arts and Sciences of Middlesex University, Cheskis played a crucial role in establishing a new Jewish-sponsored university on the campus of the former medical college.

During 1945 a group of communal leaders, hoping to revive the dream, began to explore the feasibility of establishing a new American university under Jewish auspices. Most dedicated to the idea was Rabbi Israel Goldstein, spiritual head of B'nai Jeshurun Congregation in New York. As president of the Zionist Organization of America and the Synagogue Council of America, Rabbi Goldstein had extensive organizational experience and important contacts in national communal circles.

Labor leader Joseph Schlossberg, retired secretary-treasurer of the Amalgamated Clothing Workers of America, was familiar with Rabbi Goldstein and with Dr. Joseph Cheskis, Dean of the College of Arts and Sciences of Middlesex University, a medical and veterinary school facing serious difficulties. At Mr. Schlossberg's suggestion, on January 7, 1946, the General Counsel of Middlesex, C. Ruggles Smith, wrote Rabbi Goldstein of the problems threatening the future of the university. A letter from Dr. Cheskis followed two days later. In an attempt to save their school, Mr. Smith and Dr. Cheskis were offering the Middlesex charter and campus to an appropriate group pledged to maintaining the school's nondiscriminatory admissions policy and to saving its imperilled medical college.

In his letter to Rabbi Goldstein, Mr. Smith described the nearly 100-acre Middlesex campus in Waltham, Massachusetts as "a plant admirably designed for its needs." Rabbi Goldstein visited Middlesex and later recalled his first impression in his book, *Brandeis University: Chapter of Its Founding*, published in 1951: "Poverty and bad luck had lain their imprint upon the campus. . . . It was natural, permanent grandeur marred by exigencies of impecuniousness." But he also saw the possibilities: "I was sure that this campus was intrinsically worthy of becoming the site of a great Jewish-sponsored university."

Middlesex University traced its history to 1849 and the founding and chartering of the Worcester Medical Institution by a group of Uxbridge, Massachusetts physicians. Worcester Medical remained in operation until the outbreak of the Civil War when its facilities were converted for use as an Army hospital. For decades only the school's charter survived until 1914 when Boston physician John Hall Smith [the father of C. Ruggles Smith] was elected to the board of trustees. Dr. Smith revived Worcester Medical, moving the institution to new teaching and medical facilities in Cambridge, and renaming it Middlesex College of Medicine and Surgery to reflect its

A rare snapshot of three generations of the Smith family of Middlesex University, ca. 1932. Left to right: Dr. John Hall Smith, founder of Middlesex; his son C. Ruggles Smith, Middlesex president and general counsel and first Brandeis registrar and director of admissions; grandson Richard Stacy Smith, Brandeis '54.

new location. Under Dr. Smith's direction, the school prospered, expanding as land and buildings became available. In 1917 the state established a two-year premedical program for Middlesex. Chartered as the University of Massachusetts and situated in the Back Bay area of Boston, the school also conducted classes in podiatry and pharmacy.

By 1928 enrollment had so increased that Dr. Smith began to look for a new home for the growing medical school. A tract of nearly 100 acres, the former Baker Estate, Edgecliff Park, in the neighboring suburb of Waltham, was purchased. With a new campus to plan and build, Dr. Smith relinquished his private medical practice, moved his residence to the school, and for more than ten years personally directed a crew of local workers and artisans in the construction of a university plant. The most eccentric of Smith's Middlesex structures, the medical school facilities, were fashioned from local rock, fitted with second-hand windows and fixtures, and embellished with glass and other decorative bits. The Castle, as it became known, still stands as a symbol of the institution that created it and the new university that has been its salvation.

The Middlesex Medical College catalogues detailed a program in "eclectic medicine," a course of study antithetical to what Dr. Smith (and others) viewed as the narrow sectarianism of the medical establishment of their day. Dr. Smith had long battled medical parochialism, emending the Middlesex charter to include the following: "No officer of instruction . . . shall be required by the trustees to profess any particular religious opinions as a test of office, and no student shall be refused admission to or denied any of the privileges, honors, or degrees of said college on account of the religious opinions he may entertain." Middlesex became a haven for those excluded from other institutions by religious and ethnic quotas and later recruited faculty from the wave of European educators and physicians fleeing Nazism.

In 1937 the charters of Middlesex Medical and the University of Massachusetts were merged to establish Middlesex University, empowered to confer degrees in arts, sciences, medicine, podiatry, chiropody, and veterinary medicine. The University of Massachusetts name returned to the Commonwealth to be revived later for the state institution in Amherst. With the authority to open a school of veterinary medicine, in 1938 Dr. Smith undertook building the new program, using his family's financial resources to hire faculty and construct additional facilities. By the early 1940s, the

enrollment of 200 students in the veterinary school seemed to augur a better future for Middlesex. In time, however, the entrance of America into World War II forced Middlesex into offering an accelerated one-year veterinary course and the termination of the wartime deferment for medical and veterinary students drained the school of its last resources.

In the end, there were many explanations for the Middlesex difficulties, from the unwavering commitment to an admissions policy of nondiscrimination and Dr. Smith's long battle with the medical establishment to the unsuccessful struggle to achieve financial stability and accreditation. John Hall Smith died in 1944 after devoting much of his life and his family's finances to building and sustaining his educational vision.

In reality, therefore, the institution that was being offered to Rabbi Goldstein and his supporters was a school with a promising but still unaccredited veterinary program and a medical charter in danger of revocation. Mindful of these obstacles, Rabbi Goldstein reviewed several other possible sites for the new university. It was apparent, however, that the Waltham medical school offered the best opportunity. An existing charter and a campus with room for expansion would greatly diminish the time and resources required for such an undertaking. With the assistance of a group of prominent New York supporters and Boston attorney and communal leader George Alpert, Rabbi Goldstein moved forward with plans for assuming the Middlesex campus and charter.

A first-rank institution was envisioned from the start. To secure prominent academic and communal sponsorship, Rabbi Goldstein sought the endorsement of America's most renowned scientist. In a letter dated January 22, 1946 from Princeton, Albert Einstein gave his reply: "[I will] do anything in my power to help in the creation and guidance of such an institute. It would always be near my heart."

Einstein further agreed to lend his name to a foundation that would serve as the fund-raising and public relations vehicle for the new university. On February 25, 1946,

4

the Albert Einstein Foundation for Higher Learning was chartered in the State of Delaware. As hoped, the Einstein name attracted the attention and support of many prominent figures in communal circles. The new university also received the endorsement of several important Massachusetts educators and community and government leaders, most notably Karl Compton, president of the Massachusetts Institute of Technology; Daniel Marsh, president of Boston University; Archbishop Richard Cushing of the Boston Archdiocese; and Massachusetts governor Maurice Tobin.

In the meanwhile, the new Middlesex Board of Trustees continued with the transfer of authority to the new group while Rabbi Goldstein and Mr. Alpert fought the revocation of the Middlesex medical school charter by the Massachusetts legislature. The bill to revoke was finally withdrawn on March 11, 1946 and a new Middlesex Board of Trustees was constituted.

Rabbi Goldstein and his supporters soon recognized that a new name and identity would be indispensable to the success of the venture, serving to separate the institution of the future from the medical school of the past. There was nearly unanimous support for naming the new university for Supreme Court Justice Louis Dembitz Brandeis, the distinguished American jurist who had died in 1941, bequeathing a legacy of integrity, compassion, dedication, and achievement. With the permission and support of the Brandeis family, the name Brandeis University was adopted and plans progressed for enrolling students in October 1947. Another year would pass, however, before Brandeis University opened its doors.

In an undertaking as complex as founding a modern university, dissension and disagreement often follow early unanimity. These "growing pains" – ideological conflicts, personal animosities, and power struggles – materialized as plans for the school were advancing. In September 1946, only months after launching the effort, Rabbi Goldstein resigned. Mr. Alpert and his Boston supporters continued to work with Dr. Einstein and his liaisons to the Einstein Foundation, Otto Nathan and Ralph Lazrus, until further discord led to the withdrawal of Dr. Einstein and the remaining members of the New York group. The responsibility for sustaining the vision fell to Mr. Alpert and the Boston contingent. From this group emerged seven men committed to joining Mr. Alpert in founding a university.

With Mr. Alpert as chairman, the first Brandeis University Board of Trustees was made up of six Boston business leaders – James Axelrod, Joseph Ford, Meyer Jaffe, Norman Rabb, Abraham Shapiro, and Morris Shapiro – and a former member of the Middlesex Board of Trustees, Dudley Kimball. Though neither educators nor administrators, only three with college educations, the members of the first board, both individually and collectively, shared the profound personal commitment and uncompromising dedication that would sustain them in the difficult work ahead.

Continuing where the New York sponsors had left off, the new board of trustees established the Brandeis Foundation to maintain the fund-raising and public relations functions begun by the Einstein organization. A new Educational Advisory Committee was appointed, its members chosen from the highest echelons of American education – Stephen Freeman of Middlebury College, Louis Hacker of Columbia, Hubert Heffner of Stanford, Leonard Bernstein, Paul Klapper of Queens College, Abram L. Sachar of B'nai B'rith Hillel, and attorney Susan Brandeis Gilbert.

During the succeeding months, the memberships of both the board of trustees and the Educational Advisory Committee shifted, with the major commitment for advising the trustees and establishing educational goals assumed by Dr. Klapper of Queens College and White House advisor and Boston communal leader, David Niles. The new Advisory Committee proposed to the trustees a broad set of guidelines for the university including recommendations on use of the existing campus and plans for future expansion as well as a model for the academic structure.

The most pressing matter before the board, however, was the appointment of a university president. Several qualified candidates were reviewed before Mr. Niles suggested Mr. Alpert and the trustees meet with Educational Advisory Committee member Dr. Abram Sachar, who had only recently retired as national director of Hillel and who was actively involved in planning the new university. Educated at Washington University, Harvard, and Cambridge, this former professor and historian possessed the academic credentials, personal commitment, and strength of character that would be needed for meeting the challenges ahead. In his introduction of the new president to a gathering of Boston supporters, Mr. Alpert observed: "Nature has been bountiful to Dr. Sachar, and his natural gifts, developed and enriched by training and experience, have blended in him a magnificent union of uncommon qualities. . . . He has earned the confidence and respect of the educational world."

Accepting the responsibilities, Dr. Sachar presented his personal vision of the University: "Brandeis will always strive for the highest standards. Faculty will always be chosen on the basis of capacity and potential creativity. No candidate will ever be judged by his race or his creed or his color. Students too will always be chosen by the yardstick of academic record. They will be taught that brilliance is no substitute for content, that manners and amenities and social poise cannot take the place of . . . 'the deep and earnest striving for truth.' Many of our great universities hew to the line of the finest American tradition. Brandeis wants to stand in this company."

The trustees granted unqualified freedom to the new president and his administration in the running of the academic affairs of the school. They also supported expansion of the board to reflect a national constituency and guaranteed financial solvency for the first years of university development.

The goal articulated by the Advisory Committee and the administration was to establish a small, high-caliber liberal arts institution avoiding what Justice Brandeis had called "the curse of bigness." The new university would be large enough to offer a wide range of educational opportunities and small enough to foster a sense of community. There would be no attempt to open with a full student body, but instead, by admitting one class each year, a full student enrollment would be in place at the end of a four-year undergraduate cycle. The Advisory Committee recommended deferring consideration of graduate programs until the first undergraduate degrees had been awarded and delayed a decision on the fate of the Middlesex Medical School. After a year had passed, however, the University community was so earnestly committed to the creation of the finest undergraduate institution possible with the resources available that there was little left to support a medical program of equal caliber.

The Advisory Committee also drafted criteria for the selection of faculty, seeking a community of teacher-scholars chosen for the quality of their teaching and their dedication to individual scholarship. Included in their proposals were recommendations for senior faculty to conduct introductory as well as advanced courses and guidelines that set an ideal student-teacher ratio of ten to one. These standards were accepted as the Brandeis model.

The fledgling institution was presented an enormous challenge in fashioning a faculty of the caliber outlined by the Advisory Committee. A bold approach was required, one that necessitated the shattering of a few time-honored academic traditions. The Brandeis administration met the challenge, assembling a seemingly unlikely combination of talents and personalities: experienced scholars nearing or entering retirement and bright and energetic young professors awaiting tenure in traditional academic settings. Those joining the first faculty must have seemed intellectual adventurers, chancing promising careers on an untried institution or delaying retirement for the uncertainties of an educational experiment.

The founding members of the Brandeis faculty were, in academic rank: Ludwig Lewisohn, professor of comparative literature; David Berkowitz, associate professor of history and political science; Osborne Earle, assistant professor of English; Aron Gurwitsch, assistant professor of mathematics; Milton Hindus, assistant professor of English; Lois Rossignol Mayper, assistant professor of speech and counselor of students; Joseph Cheskis, former professor and dean at Middlesex, lecturer in

Romance languages and literature; Stuart Mayper, instructor in chemistry; Shlomo Marenof, lecturer in Near Eastern languages and civilizations; Daniel Skinner, visiting lecturer in Romance languages; Reinhold Schumann, teaching fellow in history; Isaay Stempnitzky, teaching fellow in mathematics and resident proctor; William Leibowitz, assistant librarian and member of the faculty; and Ellen Lane, resident proctor and member of the faculty.

As the Advisory Committee and the administration continued to devote time and energy to creating the academy, the board of trustees and members of the Brandeis Foundation were deeply involved in efforts to garner national support for the new university. Important relationships with the press were sustained as bulletins were dispatched announcing every achievement and anticipating each development. The media campaign succeeded in drawing national attention to the new school. In the meanwhile, Mr. Alpert and the members of the board of trustees traveled the country to ensure that the new institution became not only a national news story, but also a national responsibility. This was still a university without students or a resident faculty or alumni. In a short time the American Jewish community mobilized and the Brandeis "foster alumni" were born.

The "foster alumni" or Brandeis Associates became the school's support system, a national network of members and chapters from Atlanta to Los Angeles led by the enthusiastic and resourceful Boston membership. This diverse group of supporters contributed their time, their energy, and their financial resources to a university that had yet to enroll a single student. Together with the board of trustees, the trustees' building committee, and the Brandeis Foundation, the foster alumni turned a former medical and veterinary school into a modern university.

Through the years, the members of the Brandeis Board of Trustees and the foster family have remained steadfast in their support, transforming a 100-acre site with a handful of buildings into a contemporary campus of more than 250 acres and nearly 100 buildings. For four decades their personal commitment and dedication have sustained Brandeis from accomplishment to accomplishment. In a 1956 article on Brandeis, *Time* magazine paid tribute to the foster alumni, those individuals who "gave as generously as if it had been their own alma mater." In many ways it was, and still is.

During the summer of 1948, with the first students arriving in the fall, Mr. Alpert, with his wife's encouragement, persuaded Boston communal leader Mrs. Harry Michaels to organize a women's auxiliary for Brandeis. Mrs. Michaels met with seven Boston-area women active in communal work and the Brandeis University National Women's Committee was born. The eight founders – Mrs. Harry G. Michaels, Mrs. Irving Abrams, Mrs. George Alpert, Mrs. Max Katz, Mrs. Max Ritvo, Mrs. Hyman Silverman, Mrs. Carl Spector, and Mrs. Tillie Thorner – were given the responsibility for establishing and maintaining the library. They accepted the task and pledged to build Brandeis " . . . a library on a par with the finest university libraries in America."

By the time the first students arrived on campus in October, the Women's Committee had filled the shelves of the first library, once a Middlesex University stable, with books and periodicals for an entering freshman class. In the next two years the efforts of the Women's Committee increased the library's resources ten-fold; by 1953 funds were raised for the addition of a much-needed new wing. In time, the library would play an important role in the University's successful pursuit of academic accreditation.

In the first days, the Women's Committee seemed to gain loyal followers as rapidly as it gathered books, its membership reaching 16,000 in forty-nine chapters in two years. Susan Brandeis Gilbert, daughter of the Justice and a member of the Brandeis Educational Advisory Committee, was appointed the first honorary chairperson. Later, the Brandeis University National Women's Committee became known as the largest "friends of a library" organization in the country.

Over the years, the role of the Women's Committee has evolved, mirroring the development and maturation of the University. In four decades, a small group of local supporters has grown into an organized national network of nearly 60,000 members supporting a diverse range of local and national activities, including a continuing education program. The Women's Committee has also become an important fund raiser in support of University development. The library remains, however, the Women's Committee's first responsibility.

As the campus was made ready for the start of classes, the admissions office was recruiting the first students. Brochures were mailed to 12,000 headmasters and school principals across the country. The applications returned slowly at first. But, in a short time, with the assistance of the University public relations office and the foster family, the name Brandeis became more widely known. By the second week of October 1948, the University awaited the arrival of the 107 members of the Class of 1952.

On October 7, 1948, one week before the start of classes, with the pomp and ceremony of academic tradition, Brandeis University was inaugurated and its first president installed. Attending the ceremonies in Boston's Symphony Hall were more than 200 representatives of academia.

As Dr. Sachar formally accepted the honor and the responsibility of the first Brandeis presidency, he set the course for the University: "Brandeis will be an institution of quality, where the integrity of learning, of research, of writing, will not be compromised. Brandeis University will be a school of the spirit – a school in which the temper and climate of the mind will take precedence over the acquisition of skills, and the development of techniques. Brandeis will be a dwelling place of permanent values – those few unchanging values of beauty, of righteousness, of freedom, which man has ever sought to attain. Brandeis will offer its opportunities to all. Neither student body nor faculty will ever be chosen on the basis of population proportions, whether ethnic or religious or economic."

A new chapter had begun.

Middlesex students and faculty at the Castle, ca. 1938. Photograph was used by the Einstein Foundation in early fund-raising materials with the following caption: "This is the main building of the University at Waltham, Mass., supported by the Albert Einstein Foundation for Higher Learning, Inc. It admits students of all races and creeds, without quota. Contributions are welcomed, and may be addressed to the Albert Einstein Foundation for Higher Learning, Inc., 150 Broadway, New York City."

OPPOSITE:
Press release of March 18, 1947: "Formula for Brandeis University was the topic of discussion as world-famed scientist, Albert Einstein, yesterday (Monday, March 17th) greeted delegates of the New England Associates of Brandeis University. Gathered at the physicist's home in Princeton, N. J., the group made final plans for their dinner meeting at the Hotel Somerset, Boston, on Thursday, March 20. Left to right (front row): Abraham Shapiro, George Alpert, Professor Einstein, S. Ralph Lazrus, Norman S. Rabb; (back row): Sidney H. Rabinowitz, James J. Axelrod,

Barnett D. Gordon, Robert P. Cable, Yoland D. Markson, and Irving Usen." Four members of this group later helped to form the founding board of trustees of Brandeis University – George Alpert, James J. Axelrod, Norman S. Rabb, and Abraham Shapiro.

10

"As we met in 1947 and 1948, only seven men came regularly. These are the men who today are recognized as the original founding trustees. I was fortunate to have been one of this group. Others in the group were George Alpert, James Axelrod, Joseph Ford, Meyer Jaffe, Abraham Shapiro, Morris Shapiro; later, Dudley Kimball, a Harvard graduate and associate of Dr. Smith's, joined the group to make it eight founding trustees. The meetings were held in Abraham Shapiro's offices – The Gold Seal Rubber Company on Lincoln Street in Boston. Shapiro made his very nice boardroom available. . . . The meetings were often stormy. Many times I felt that our dream would never come to fruition. I believe it is safe to say that if it were not for Abraham Shapiro, there would not have been a Brandeis. He would calm the atmosphere by banging on the table and asking, 'Are you here to argue and fight or to build a university?'"

NORMAN S. RABB
Founding Member, Board of Trustees

The former home of the president of Middlesex University went through several incarnations on the Brandeis campus. First known as University Hall, it was renamed Woodruff Hall in 1952 and housed the office of the president and other administrative units, ca. 1952.

Inspection of early campus renovations, ca. 1948. Left to right: Professor David Berkowitz, director of university planning; Jacob Shapiro, Brandeis trustee; George Alpert, chairman, Brandeis Board of Trustees; Archie Riskin, architect; and Meyer Jaffe, chairman, Brandeis Trustees' Building Committee.

A Middlesex medical laboratory in the Castle, ca. 1935. During the months preceding the opening of Brandeis, the administration and foster alumni were busy transforming a former medical college into a modern university.

The metamorphosis complete, the former Middlesex medical laboratory became a popular and functional commons room for Brandeis students, ca. 1948.

Left to right: Brandeis University Board of Trustees Chairman George Alpert, President Abram Sachar, and Rabbi Israel Goldstein at University inaugural festivities, October 7–8, 1948. Rabbi Goldstein organized early efforts to found a Jewish-sponsored nonsectarian university following World War II and enlisted the support of Albert Einstein.

President Sachar's induction address in Symphony Hall, October 7, 1948. Guests on stage behind podium, left to right: Nelson Glueck, president, Hebrew Union College–Jewish Institute of Religion; Arthur H. Compton, chancellor, Washington University; George Alpert, chairman, Brandeis University Board of Trustees; Eliahu Elath, Head of the Special Mission of the State of Israel to the United States; Dudley Kimball and Joseph Ford, founding trustees, Brandeis University.

University marshal and founding faculty member Osborne Earle, leading academic procession at the University inauguration in Symphony Hall, Boston, October 7, 1948.

Susan Brandeis Gilbert at exhibition of Brandeisiana in University library during inaugural festivities. Special loans on view included portraits of Justice Brandeis, original manuscripts from the University of Louisville, and personal papers of the Brandeis family, October 7–8, 1948.

The first Brandeis library, once a Middlesex University stable, ca. 1948. The members of the Brandeis University National Women's Committee filled the shelves of the first campus library with books and periodicals suitable for the entering freshman class.

*Original Brandeis library with
new wing added to accommodate
growing University collection,
ca. 1953. The rapid development
of the library was the result of the
continuing efforts and support of
the membership of the Brandeis
University National Women's
Committee.*

OPPOSITE:
*Coeds on the steps of the first library,
ca. 1953. Among the new materials
for the collection was a recording
of* Appalachian Spring *by Aaron
Copland, a member of the Brandeis
Advisory Committee on Educational
Policies in Music.*

*Seven of the eight founders of
the Brandeis University National
Women's Committee, ca. 1948. Left
to right: Mrs. Max Katz, Mrs. Max
Ritvo, Mrs. Harry Michaels, Mrs.
Irving Abrams, Mrs. Carl Spector,
Mrs. Hyman Silverman, and Mrs.
Tillie Thorner. (Not pictured, Mrs.
George Alpert.)*

*"In the third year of the University, I met at the National Office
(then in downtown Boston), with a man who wished to see me.
He unfolded the following story: he was a factory worker who
had read the publicity about this new university and was greatly
impressed and proud. His employer, who had heard me speak at a
meeting, told him he had enrolled his daughter as a Life Member
(then $100) in the Women's Committee. This man had come with
$100 and wished to become a Life Member. I explained that the
University and the Women's Committee were founded upon and
embraced democratic principles, but the Committee was limited
to women. Finally, with an indescribable sadness, he said: 'I have
no wife, no children, no brothers or sisters – no family. Isn't there
some place I can put my name so that when I am gone it will show
that I was here?' The poignancy of this was overwhelming, and I
told him that we could do something, that we would establish a
Book Collection, every volume of which would bear his name.
Although he was untutored, he was an avid reader with biography
his great interest, and this was the field we chose. This man's wish
for perpetuity became the forerunner of all the various book
collections, ranging from $100-$5,000, continuing to this day to
bring in millions of dollars to the Libraries."*

HANNAH W. ABRAMS
*Founder, Brandeis University National Women's Committee,
President, 1951–1953*

Founding faculty member Ludwig
Lewisohn, professor of comparative
literature, posed with his beloved cat
Cupcake and students in his Castle
apartment for the Boston Sunday
Herald, *May 29, 1949. Courtesy
Boston Herald. Following his death
in 1955, Brandeis students paid
tribute to the beloved critic, author,
and teacher by establishing the
Ludwig Lewisohn Memorial
Lecture Series.*

*President and Mrs. Sachar at home
with students, ca. 1950.*

Photograph appearing in the January 18, 1949 issue of Look *magazine was captioned: "Dr. David Berkowitz conducts history seminar against skeleton background, a leftover from days when buildings housed a medical school." Courtesy* Look *magazine. Photograph strikingly captured the early transition from medical school to liberal arts university.*

Brandeis student spirit reached a
peak with "Boost Brandeis Week,"
1950. This pose epitomized for many
the quintessential American college
experience of the early 1950s.

OPPOSITE:
An early campus landmark, the
wishing well in winter, ca. 1949.

PAGES 26-27:
The Class of '52 in Usen Commons
Room, ca. spring 1952.

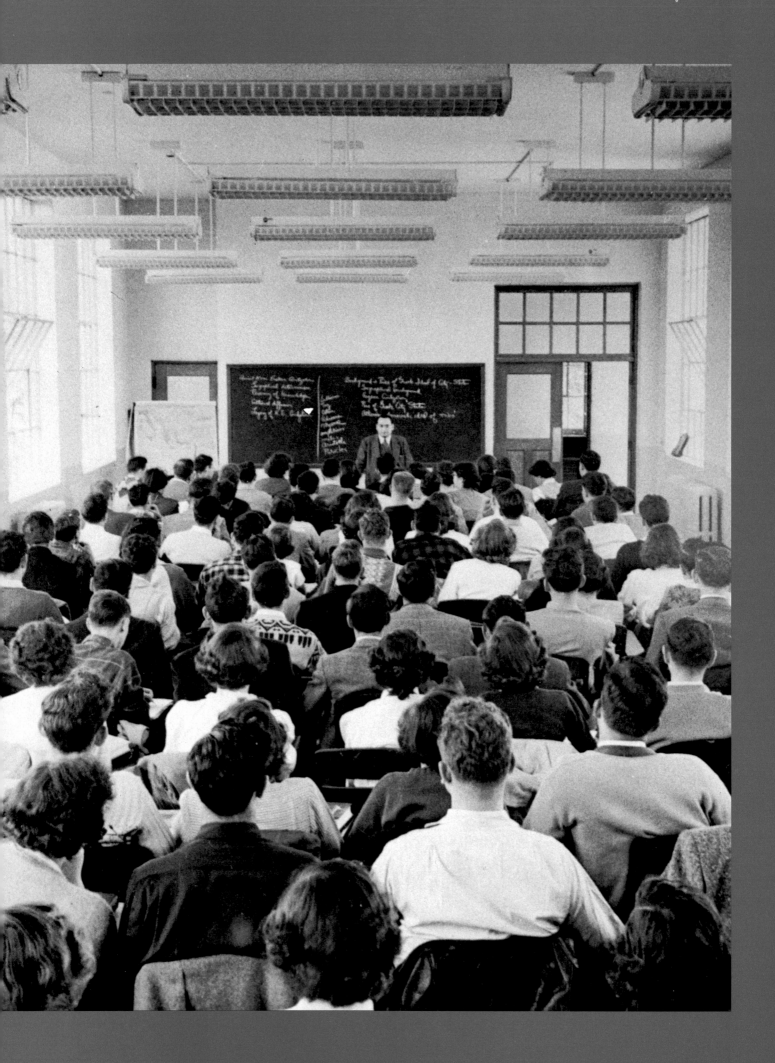

THE EARLY YEARS

"A Young University in a Hurry"

"The achievements made at Brandeis University in its short history represent a phenomenon deserving of a special chapter in the history of mid-twentieth-century American higher education."

NILS Y. WESSELL

President, Tufts University, announcing accreditation by the New England Association of Colleges and Secondary Schools, December 8, 1953

With perseverance and dedication the founders of Brandeis had advanced the dream. But the dramatic beginnings were just the prologue; the real challenge still lay ahead. Establishing a modern university required more than devotion and commitment; it also demanded considerable organizational skill and vast financial resources.

When the first students arrived on campus in October 1948, the administration began implementation of the academic guidelines. The Educational Advisory Committee had studied several traditional and innovative designs before determining that the best model would be that of a small liberal arts institution with neither an experimental nor a vocational approach to undergraduate education. The early catalogues outlined a simple, but farsighted plan, designed to "transform the novice into the thinker." The University was divided into four schools: general studies, social science, science, and humanities, with a fifth, the school of music, drama, and fine arts, scheduled to open in the second year. All Brandeis students matriculated in the School of General Studies before undertaking a concentration in one of the University's "upper" divisions. The stated goal of this general education plan was to ensure that all students were introduced to "the major experience of our social evolution and to those significant scientific achievements which should be the common possession of educated men and women."

In designing the Brandeis academy, the administration had recognized early that the young university did not have the luxury of time. The postwar educational system called for immediate realization of critical standards and almost overnight attainment of academic recognition. By the end of the first year, Brandeis credits were accepted for transfer by the New York State Department of Education. In 1951, the Commonwealth of Massachusetts authorized Brandeis to confer graduate and professional degrees and to acquire resources free of statutory limits.

As daily concerns continued to focus on allocating slender resources for an increasingly expensive program of university development and expansion, external

OPPOSITE: *Social Science A with Dr. David Berkowitz, ca. 1951.*

pressures intruded. Before achieving full enrollment, Brandeis faced the possibility of losing half its student body to conscription in the Korean Conflict. But the business of education proceeded without interruption as students and administration followed the advice of President Sachar to "prepare for the worst and live for the best." The announcement of the student deferment by President Truman on April 1, 1951, in a sense saved the future of Brandeis.

The achievements of these early years can be seen in the rapid increases in numbers of students, faculty, staff, and facilities. The faculty doubled by the second year and reached eighty-four by the first commencement and more than 150 by the end of the first decade. Similarly, the student body of 107 grew to 244 in 1949, 651 in 1952, and totalled 1,100 undergraduates in 1958. But dramatic growth did not preclude the continued pursuit of excellence: the low student-faculty ratio was maintained despite geometric increases in enrollment. And programs designed to foster a sense of community proliferated.

As the University grew, the Brandeis Board of Trustees also expanded and diversified to represent a truly national constituency. The eight founding trustees expanded the board in succeeding years to include as many as fifty members, whose importance to the University's continued growth and development cannot be overstated. In 1951 the trustees established the Board of Fellows with the Honorable Herbert Lehman, United States Senator from New York, serving as the first honorary chairman and attorney Frank L. Weil as chairman. Forty years later, the Brandeis Board of Fellows is made up of nearly 400 national leaders from business, education, the law and public life.

The administration's commitment to fashioning a faculty of talented teacher-scholars did not diminish with time, but intensified as the University continued to

recruit distinguished candidates for faculty positions. The promise of scholarly careers in departments unfettered by archaic traditions proved attractive to many who left more established institutions for the adventure of Brandeis. Even in the early years of few resources, the University was able to recruit many eminent scholars: Albert Guérard, Max Lerner, Frank Manuel, Abraham Maslow, and Nahum Glatzer joined the early faculty together with promising younger academicians including Leonard Levy, Irving Fine, Saul Cohen, Svend Laursen, Irving Howe, James Duffy, Lewis Coser, Ricardo Morant, Harry Zohn, and Robert Manners.

While the Brandeis faculty and administration were devoting their time to establishing and implementing the University's academic programs, the first undergraduates were busy developing the extracurricular activities considered essential to American college life. The earliest brochures outlined a variety of student groups planned for the new campus; but the administration had underestimated the enthusiasm and resourcefulness of the early classes. In the first year, the Class of '52 organized a life outside the classroom that included the first student newspaper, *The Justice*; a literary publication, *The Turret*; a choral society; groups for drama, French, semantics, and film; the Outing Club; and a chapter of the Collegiate Council of the United Nations. Each succeeding group of students expanded the range of activities and before long the campus had an astronomy society, a debating club, a yearbook committee, pre-law and pre-med groups, a Gilbert and Sullivan society, a modern dance club, several religious groups, a chapter of Students for Democratic Action, and the Hi Charlie Review, a popular organization responsible for presenting musical parodies of University policies, faculty, and administration, written, composed, produced, directed, and acted by students. It was often observed that there were more clubs than students to join them.

In 1949, to provide for the "healthy educational experience of the students,"

Brandeis organized an athletic program and named former University of Michigan football All-American Benny Friedman as director. With his staff, Friedman developed the first football squad, the Brandeis "team of destiny," named with perhaps more hope than expectation. Other "teams of destiny" soon followed in basketball, soccer, and baseball. To assist the new effort, the Brandeis University Athletic Association was formed under the enthusiastic leadership of Trustee Joseph Linsey. The Abraham Shapiro Athletic Center and the Abraham Marcus Playing Field were among the first facilities added to the campus and in 1967 the Joseph Linsey Sports Center was built.

But the role of intercollegiate athletics became a topic of vigorous campus debate. The funds and personnel needed to maintain a varsity program had to be measured against the increasing costs of the University's growing academic commitments and rapidly developing physical plant. The "team of destiny" played its last season of football in the 1959–1960 academic year and was subsequently replaced by a more diverse, and less financially draining, schedule of intercollegiate and intramural sports.

Over the years athletics has remained an integral part of the Brandeis educational experience guided by a staff of dedicated coaches and athletic directors, including Harry Stein, Walter Mahoney, K. C. Jones, Irv Olin, Lisel Judge, Nick Rodis, Norm Levine, and Jeff Cohen. Brandeis has gained national collegiate honors for individual and team competition in soccer, basketball, tennis, track, and fencing. In 1987 the continuing search to find an appropriate role for athletics on a decidedly academic campus was finally resolved when Brandeis was elected to the new University Athletic Association, a national organization whose members include such institutions as the University of Chicago, Emory University, and Carnegie-Mellon.

Surely the most visible indication of the University's early growth and development was the dramatic transformation of the campus beginning with the modernization of the former Middlesex structures. With the cooperation of local architects, engi-

Brandeis foster alumni reviewing the first University Master Plan submitted by Saarinen, Saarinen and Associates, November 1950. Harold Sherman Goldberg (left) was Chairman of the Board of the Greater Boston Chapter of the Brandeis University Associates.

One of the first new buildings added to the campus was the Abraham Shapiro Athletic Center, named for the founding trustee, ca. 1953.

neers, and construction firms, the campus was being readied for the first students even as they arrived. The Class of 1952 was educated, fed, and housed in a handful of refurbished Middlesex buildings. The efforts and generosity of the foster family turned a medical school laboratory into an attractive commons room and army surplus buildings into women's dormitories. Dr. Smith's Castle saw new life as a men's dormitory, dining hall, and small infirmary.

Before long, however, it was clear that more space would be needed to accommodate the increasing enrollment. A trustees' building committee headed by Meyer Jaffe was set up to oversee campus development and founding faculty member Dr. David Berkowitz was appointed director of the Office of University Planning with responsibility for studying and surveying the campus to find short-term solutions for classroom and living needs and a plan for future development. In setting up mechanisms for long-range planning, the goal was to avoid random and haphazard growth and in so doing create a new and special architectural character. In an amazingly short time, the Brandeis landscape would reflect Rabbi Goldstein's early vision of "what a glorious place this campus could become."

In April 1949 the board of trustees engaged architect Eero Saarinen, whose name was widely recognized for the design of educational institutions. The firm of Saarinen, Saarinen, and Associates was hired to create a campus master plan. In the meantime, however, work continued on facilities for incoming students. The Ridgewood Quadrangle was built in 1950 by Boston architect Archie Riskin and two parts of the Saarinen-designed Hamilton Quadrangle (later renamed Massell) were completed in January 1952.

The Saarinen plan was submitted in 1952 and the Brandeis campus still bears the imprint of the first master design. Among the most notable of Saarinen's contributions are the irregular clusters of buildings low in scale, surrounded by open areas. Dormitory quadrangles are sited on the periphery, creating an intentional and striking separation between areas of instruction and student residences. The natural landscape has been incorporated into the campus architecture with structures growing out of the many natural rocky ledges. And the "towers and battlements" of the Castle remain as links between the present and the past, for as Saarinen had observed, the Castle was like the rocks, "it belonged to the terrain."

Responsibility for the Brandeis master plan was subsequently assumed by the architectural firm of Harrison and Abramovitz. In 1955 Max Abramovitz was appointed University architectural counsel and a year later, master planner. Under his direction, thirty-five new structures were completed by the end of the first decade. The earliest Harrison and Abramovitz buildings included Ullman Amphitheatre, Slosberg Music Center, Mailman Hall (now Morton May Memorial Hall), Stoneman Infirmary, and the first Rabb Graduate Center (now Pearlman Hall). Over the next several years the firm directed the construction of buildings of its own design as well as those of other architectural firms including Shepley, Bulfinch, Richardson, and Abbott; The Architects Collaborative (Benjamin Thompson); and Hugh Stubbins and Associates.

Abramovitz, like Saarinen before him, gave careful thought to the relationship between campus architecture and University philosophy, planning, in his words, "... a unique and naturalistic campus pattern conducive to the personal ideals of teaching the University stands for. This architectural character is felt to be consistent with the intimate, humane, and personal educational approach that Brandeis has been developing."

Perhaps the single most dramatic architectural commission was the 1955 Harrison and Abramovitz design of the chapels. To appropriately fulfill the University's needs, the firm designed three structures of equal height and size but different appearance with exteriors unadorned by religious symbols and interiors planned to meet the specific requirements of each faith. No building casts shadows on another and the separation of the chapels from the rest of the campus by the Chapel Field Area creates a sense of isolation and serenity reserved for worship and contemplation.

The construction and dedication of the Berlin, Bethlehem, and Harlan chapels followed an extended debate by the administration, trustees, and students over the role of religion and religious representations at Brandeis. Several designs were discussed before a consensus was reached that supported the construction of three separate sanctuaries with funds raised privately within each of the denominations represented. The dedication ceremonies were highlighted by the awarding of honorary degrees to Justice John Marshall Harlan, whose grandfather's name was given to the Protestant chapel, and to theologians Paul Tillich, Jacques Maritain, and Leo Baeck. In the end, the Brandeis chapels received widespread attention — awards for architectural design and praise for a new model for religious structures on American college campuses.

But it was more than architectural innovation that brought national recognition to the young institution. In a 1949 article, *Time* magazine referred to the new university as "ambitious little Brandeis." Indeed, the school was rapidly developing as a hothouse of activity, a lively community of students, faculty, and administration. Much of this early excitement had been born of necessity.

Because the University was still developing and resources were slender, an adjunct faculty of visiting creative artists, scientists, philosophers, social scientists, and poets were invited to supplement regular classroom offerings. Under the auspices of innovative programs, the foremost personalities of the day came to Brandeis to participate in a variety of activities: as lecturers in General Education S and the Institute of Adult Education, as Ziskind Visiting Professors, as convocation speakers, and as guests in early lecture series honoring Justice Brandeis, Ambassador Abba Eban, labor leader Sidney Hillman, and Rabbi Stephen Wise. This visiting army of intellectuals included important contributors to mid-twentieth-century thought, most notably Robert Maynard Hutchins, Leo Szilard, Sidney Hook, I.I. Rabi, Harlow Shapley, E. E. Cummings, Norbert Wiener, Max Weber, Alexander Meiklejohn, Erich Heller, Margaret Mead, Archibald MacLeish, and Alfred Kinsey. And despite the number and caliber of visiting faculty and guests, the costs were low, as most agreed to participate for little more than traveling expenses.

A principal vehicle for these extraordinary educational opportunities was General Education S, initiated as a "capstone" class for seniors in the 1951–1952 academic year. Distinguished guests were invited to "Gen Ed S" to speak of the influences and decisions that had shaped their lives. The series, subtitled "The Productive Life," consisted of a guest lecture followed a week later by an intense, often heated, panel discussion conducted by the faculty. The stated goal was to enable students "to analyze the basic questions underlying their choice of values in a real world" and the guests were chosen to represent a wide range of experience and outlook. In one form or

Boston attorney Joseph Welch with students following his Gen Ed S talk, December 1955. Welch gained national prominence as the Army's Special Counsel in the hearings before Senator Joseph McCarthy.

another, "Gen Ed S" remained a part of the curriculum for many years, a symbol of the quintessential Brandeis educational experience and a forum for the exploration of a variety of ideas and philosophies in an open and unrestrained manner.

A continuing infusion of new ideas from visiting scholars has been sustained for more than three decades through the auspices of the Ziskind Visiting Professorships. From the appointment of Henry Steele Commager as the first Ziskind Visiting Professor in 1954, the Brandeis experience has been enlivened by a host of visiting historians, writers, artists, philosophers, scientists, composers, and social scientists. Ziskind professors remain at the University for one semester or longer, teaching classes, leading seminars, and participating in other campus activities.

On June 16, 1952 the University's pioneering days culminated with the celebration of the first commencement and the awarding of bachelor's degrees to 102 students of the Class of 1952. The occasion was marked by Eleanor Roosevelt's commencement address and the first Brandeis Festival of the Creative Arts, organized and directed by Leonard Bernstein.

At the second commencement the following June, the University reached another milestone, graduating the Class of 1953 and awarding the University's first honorary degrees to founding board chairman George Alpert, Senator Paul Douglas, and historian Louis Ginzburg. The roll call of honorary degree recipients now totals 400 individuals who have distinguished themselves in law, politics, arts, letters, science, and philanthropy.

Despite all the early achievements and advances made by the University, the necessity of academic accreditation had remained a persistent concern. Indeed, the first two graduating classes held diplomas from an unaccredited institution. On December 8, 1953, following the required graduation of two classes and review and approval of campus library facilities, at a large meeting of University supporters in Boston, Brandeis was notified of accreditation by the New England Association of Colleges and Secondary Schools. The announcement was made by the Association's head, Tufts University president Nils Y. Wessell, who paid tribute to the distinction Brandeis had earned "only through conscientious effort and high ideals."

Academic accreditation was the first of many important endorsements by the educational community that would enable the University to abridge decades of tradition. The challenge facing Brandeis in the earliest days had been to establish as fine a school as possible with the resources available. In telling the story of these early years in a 1962 *Saturday Review* article, writer Lewis Gillenson referred to Brandeis as "the young university in a hurry," an appropriate description still of an institution that aspired to and attained excellence in a single generation.

OPPOSITE:
The University's youngest hawker holding the first edition of The Justice, March 24, 1949. *Front page articles covered mid-year examinations and plans for converting the Middlesex animal hospital to a speech clinic, as well as an interview with President Sachar on the future of the University. Over the years* The Justice *has addressed issues large and small, from the first amendment and civil rights to dormitory overcrowding and library hours.*

Students arriving for registration, September 1950. Freshman Orientation Week activities began with a welcoming dinner, receptions, and tours of Boston and ended with three grueling days of placement and diagnostic tests.

Four members of the early science faculty in Ford Hall, February 1953. Standing, left to right: Robert L. Edwards, instructor in zoology; Carl J. Sindermann, instructor in biology; Samuel J. Golub, assistant professor of biology. Seated, Albert G. Olsen, instructor in biology.

Members of the social sciences faculty, ca. 1953. Left to right: Robert A. Manners, assistant professor of anthropology; Philip Rieff, instructor in social relations; Lewis A. Coser, lecturer in the social sciences.

Early faculty often used their homes as classrooms. Here, assistant professor of English Thomas Savage conducting a class in his living room, March 1951. Novelist Savage had sold the film rights to his novel Lona Hanson *the previous year.*

"Brandeis in the early years was, as the British political scientist Gordon K. Lewis perceptively noted, a kind of 'Oxford of the mind.' Discoveries and encounters crowded the inner landscape. There were lectures by distinguished visitors: Buber, Maritain, and Tillich on religion, Justices Douglas and Frankfurter on the Constitution, David Ben-Gurion on the founding of Israel, Robert Maynard Hutchins on the sorry state of American culture. A poetry series meant weekends with W. H. Auden and Dylan Thomas. Leonard Bernstein mesmerized us with Mahler and led the thrilling American premiere of The Threepenny Opera *and his own* Trouble in Tahiti. *In Gen Ed S (for seniors), Max Lerner invited creative men and women (also known as 'role models'), including Margaret Mead, Archibald MacLeish, Leo Szilard, Alfred Kinsey, Agnes De Mille, and Norbert Wiener, to tell us of their turning points and torments. (A week later a faculty panel 'dissected' the previous week's guest and each other, to our shameless delight.)*

"We social science majors were especially privileged. American history came to us live each week from Columbia in the person of Henry Steele Commager, a bulldog who could not only stand on his hind legs and talk but give spellbinding lectures without notes for two hours straight. We read Max Weber with Lew Coser, Freud with Philip Rieff, Kant with Aron Gurwitsch, Nietzsche with Frank Manuel, Burckhardt on the Renaissance with David Berkowitz, studied civil liberties with Leonard Levy, the power elite with C. Wright Mills, psychology with Abe Maslow and Jim Klee, and Marx with practically everyone.

"Did we know we were living in a Golden Age? Of course not. We were merely amused when kindly old Jake Gilbert, the husband of Justice Brandeis's daughter Susan, sat beneath LDB's portrait in Usen Commons and tried to persuade us how fortunate we were to be attending a school created in the image of his father-in-law rather than one named for some Ivy League ne'er-do-well: 'They say John Harvard once wrote a book, but ask 'em to show it to you and they'll say it's lost; Eli Yale was just a locksmith; but Brandeis — why, he was a real thinker and a great judge.' We laughed, but old Jake was right after all. It was a special place at a special time and we were lucky to have been there when we were."

SANDY LAKOFF '53

*Max Lerner, professor of American
civilization and institutions,
February 1952. At his retirement in
1973, the distinguished author and
journalist described how he had
come to the young university "to
help open the book of history and fill
the pages not yet written upon."*

*At left, Gen Ed S speaker Dr.
Alfred Kinsey in conversation with
associate professor of psychology,
Abraham Maslow, December 5,
1952. The publication of* Sexual
Behavior in the Human Male *in 1948
had catapulted the research scientist
into the national spotlight. During
his Brandeis visit, Kinsey also met
with classes in social science,
psychology, and zoology.*

An early Gen Ed guest Margaret Mead, associate curator of ethnology, American Museum of Natural History, New York, March 14, 1952. Max Lerner introduced the noted anthropologist to the Brandeis audience as his image of the "ideal social scientist."

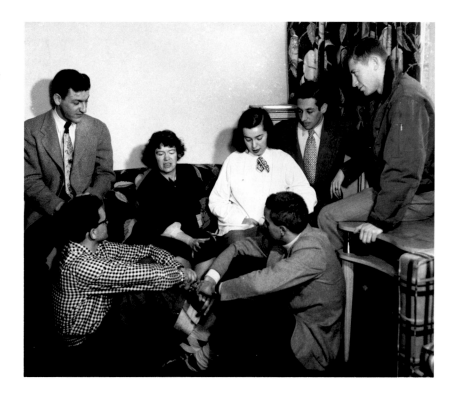

"Twenty people, rather twenty-one, including the professor, Dr. Richard Jones, were sitting in chairs in a circle in his large office in the psych center. We looked at Dr. Jones, with his pad in his lap, and waited for something to happen. Nothing at all happened for fifteen minutes until one of the students broke the ice with a comment that elicited a laugh from the others in the room. The occasion was the first session of the one-day-a-week lab that Dr. Jones conducted as part of his course on educational psychology. The class and the program were, for Brandeis, both typical and unique. Typical because professors frequently approached instruction in unorthodox fashion. Unique because there was probably at the time no other "ed. psych" course in the country being taught this way (which was also typical of Brandeis): a laboratory in which, unknowingly, for a while anyway, the class was acting out the premise described in the lectures, thus reinforcing the power of the premise and the substance of the course. The theory was that people learn academic subjects best by being able to make a connection between the material being taught and something personal to the students. The lab was demonstrating that good instruction should result in expansion of self-knowledge, while, at the same time, acting out many or most of the emotions and problems a teacher faces in a classroom and reinforcing an understanding of both processes. Thus, the students learned about themselves and the subject matter in a stimulating and memorable fashion, evidenced by the fact that twenty-five years later I can recall both those sessions and the point of the course."

RONALD L. KAISERMAN '63

The design of the three chapels at Brandeis offered a new model for the construction of religious structures on American college campuses. Berlin Chapel, July 1958. The University's Jewish chapel was donated by the friends of Boston physician Dr. David Berlin and named in honor of his parents, Mendel and Leah Berlin.

OPPOSITE:
Bethlehem Chapel, ca. 1958. The designation of the Catholic chapel was made by then Boston Archbishop Richard J. Cushing, who celebrated the first mass on September 9, 1955.

The altar of Harlan Chapel, ca. 1955. The Protestant chapel was named in honor of the late Supreme Court Justice, John Marshall Harlan, the only dissenting vote in Ferguson v. Plessy, the decision that established "separate but equal" education in America. Justice Harlan's position was finally vindicated in 1954 when the "separate but equal" principle was overturned in Brown v. Board of Education of Topeka.

Brandeis basketball coach K. C. Jones, ca. 1967. The University coaching position was the first for Jones following his retirement as a professional player for the Boston Celtics and marked the beginning of a new career. To right of Jones in photograph is Brandeis athletic director Irv Olin.

Women's field hockey class, ca. 1955.

Athletic director and football coach, Benny Friedman, being carried by his Brandeis "team of destiny," November 8, 1958. Brandeis was victorious in the 1958 homecoming game against Bridgeport.

Cheerleaders for the early "teams of destiny" in Brandeis blue and white, September 1951.

The first four Brandeis "teams of destiny," included varsity squads in football, soccer, basketball, and baseball. Here, Brandeis vs. Harvard, May 1963.

OPPOSITE:
On right, Brandeis fencing coach Lisel Judge with team member, Roberta Sigel '61, 1961. Brandeis has sent undefeated fencing teams to national collegiate competitions.

A soccer match, ca. 1976. Player on right is Cleveland Lewis, considered one of the finest Brandeis soccer players.

Folksinger Pete Seeger in concert, April 24, 1955. Seeger gave several campus performances including this one a few months prior to his appearance before the House Committee on Un-American Activities.

A meeting of the Student Council, December 1950. The Council was the representative body of the Student Union whose membership included all Brandeis undergraduates.

OPPOSITE:
Banquet honoring the University's first Dean's List, 1949. Social maturity and development notwithstanding, intellectual growth and achievement remained the raison d'etre of a Brandeis education.

"I suppose the first – and the longest-lasting – impression that there was something special about Brandeis came to me during my first visit to the school. That was in the fall of 1963 when I was invited out by Leonard Levy and John Roche to talk about coming to the history department. It was nice to meet up with such fresh and active minds; it was nice to look around the Faculty Center dining room and see what was obviously an intellectually alive group of prospective colleagues. But it was nicest of all to be confronted with the daily special: London broil with sauce béarnaise – and potato kugel. I knew right away that it was my kind of place. It still is."

MORTON KELLER
Samuel J. and Augusta Spector Professor of History

Student couples posed at work
and play in front of the library,
May 1951.

Ice skating was a popular winter activity in Kane Reflecting Pool in the Hamilton Quadrangle, ca. 1950.

A room in Roosevelt Hall, a girls' dormitory, ca. 1953. Early Brandeis publications outlined the role of campus housing in assisting students in "attaining individual resourcefulness and social maturity."

"In 1954, I came to Brandeis as a green seventeen-year-old from the Midwest, speaking with such a drawl that New Yorkers walked away before I could finish a sentence. A few years later, I'd become snotty enough to stand up at a Gen Ed session and ask the leader of Britain's Labour Party in what sense he still believed in socialism. There was an air of unreality about Brandeis in the '50s, but also a climate in which wildly individualistic teachers and students could feel that what they learned and believed in mattered. I remember a seminar where a student with a beautiful voice read the three-page story "Araby." The argument that followed lasted ninety minutes, as three professors who were among the most compelling critics of their time violently debated the merits of the story, the value of James Joyce, the nature of realistic fiction, and the history of the West. We learned that disagreement was a style of taking people seriously, and that all tastes and values implied social and historical assumptions. Imagine my shock to graduate Brandeis and find that polite company did not generally accept these premises. Life continued to surprise me, and in some ways I remained a green midwestern boy. The difference was that, after Brandeis, when disturbing events happened in the world, we could no longer call the whole community into a commons lounge and, young and old, green and ripe, fight it out together."

JEREMY LARNER '58

The functional Usen Castle
Commons Room served as lounge,
lecture hall, meeting room, and
here, as dance floor, ca. 1954.

University convocation, ca. 1950. Prior to the first Brandeis commencement in 1952, three academic convocations drew thousands to the campus to hear addresses by United Nations ambassadors Abba Eban and Ralph Bunche, Brandeis trustee Eleanor Roosevelt, and educational reformer Robert Maynard Hutchins.

"'Forty years is a whole lifetime!' said Dostoyevsky. Forty years ago, when Dr. Sachar invited me, as a young assistant professor at the University of Chicago, to join the skeletal faculty of a non-existent university, Brandeis, I could not have imagined what the future would hold in store for both of us. In retrospect, I can truly say that virtually all of my most sanguine hopes for the new institution and myself have been realized and none of my quite understandable and legitimate fears. We have thrived together and have much to be thankful for."

MILTON HINDUS
Edytha Macy Gross Professor of Humanities Emeritus

*Left to right: Student marshals
Paul Levenson, Student Union
president, and Gus Ranis, Senior
Class president, lead historic
first commencement procession,
June 16, 1952.*

BUILDING A RESEARCH UNIVERSITY

"A Center of Excellence"

"Brandeis is engaged in an historic mission: the development of a great new center of teaching and research which will make superior higher education accessible to more able young people, which will advance the frontiers of knowledge, and which, by doing these things, will enable Brandeis to take its place among the great universities of the nation and the world. There is no higher purpose to claim your allegiance and support."

JAMES W. ARMSEY
*Director of Special Programs, Ford Foundation, at the mid-season conference of Brandeis Trustees, Fellows of the University, and President's Council,
December 19, 1964*

By the first commencement in 1952, the Brandeis undergraduate program had been both strengthened and diversified. Plans for future campus expansion were progressing as student enrollment continued to surge. During this period of rapid growth and development, and continued concern over financial stability, the young institution faced critical decisions regarding its future: Brandeis could remain a small liberal arts university with a fine undergraduate college and a modest graduate school or it could evolve into a national research institution with a strong commitment to both a college and a graduate school of arts and sciences. Dean of the Brandeis Graduate School Leonard Levy compared the two traditions in an article for the *Brandeis University Bulletin* in 1962: "A college is fundamentally a teaching institution. Its purpose is to transmit, but not to advance learning. A university, by contrast, exists not merely to transmit knowledge, but to advance its boundaries. A university's central purpose is research and scholarship and its central feature is the exacting and disciplined intellectual performance called for in the Ph. D. program."

As critical discussions on the future of Brandeis began, some members of the administration and board of trustees considered it imprudent for a young liberal arts university to proceed into graduate education and research a mere five years after its establishment. Many others, however, argued that changing course later, in midstream, would be more wrenching than taking what seemed the more radical and speculative path at the outset.

Those favoring the more drastic approach noted that the explosion of research following World War II made it possible to build a high-quality university in a single generation whereas establishing a liberal arts school of equal reputation would require the passage of half a century or longer. With a faculty increasingly qualified for and interested in scholarly research and the training of graduate students, Brandeis chose the bolder, but ultimately more rewarding, course. Indeed, from its founding, the University had endeavored to fashion what Brandeis psychology professor Abraham Maslow described as a community of "working intellects – teachers who will offer instruction in fields in which they are actively at work as scholars."

In 1951 Brandeis had been granted the power to award graduate and professional degrees by the Commonwealth of Massachusetts; two years later a graduate school of arts and sciences was established, enrolling the first postbaccalaureate students in September 1953. The decision to proceed with graduate education was made early but judiciously, building programs that took advantage of existing faculty strength and depth. Initially, graduate degrees were offered in four areas, one in each of the University's "upper" schools – chemistry, music composition, Near Eastern and Judaic studies, and psychology. The first Brandeis doctorates were offered in psychology and Near Eastern and Judaic studies, with master of arts degrees in chemistry and Near Eastern and Judaic studies, and a master of fine arts degree in music. Max Lerner was named first chairman of the Brandeis Graduate School of Arts and Sciences with Saul Cohen, Simon Rawidowicz, Irving Fine, and Abraham Maslow heading the graduate committees in chemistry, Near Eastern and Judaic Studies, music composition, and psychology, respectively.

The philosophy of graduate education was described in University catalogues: "The underlying ideal of the graduate school is to assemble a community of scholars, scientists, and artists, in whose company the student-scholar can pursue studies and research as an apprentice. Degrees will be granted upon the evidence of intellectual growth and development, rather than solely on the basis of formal course credits." Inauguration of the Graduate School took place on January 14, 1954 as representatives of more than 150 universities, colleges, and learned societies gathered for ceremonies in Shapiro Athletic Center.

In the first year, forty-two graduate students matriculated. Now, as the University enters its fifth decade, there are twenty degree programs enrolling more than 600 students. Brandeis conferred its first master's degrees in 1954, its first doctorate in 1957, and since then, more than 2,000 master of arts degrees, 500 master of fine arts degrees, and 1,500 doctorates have been granted by the Graduate School of Arts and Sciences.

As the University continued to mature and develop, the simple academic and administrative structure of the early years began to yield to a more complex arrangement. While the original academic plan had been devised to avoid traditional departmental competition and to encourage and facilitate a spirit of cooperation and community among faculty, there was growing concern for the integrity of each discipline within a rapidly expanding institution. To meet the increasing needs of the faculty and academic programs, in 1955 Brandeis appointed its first dean of faculty whose responsibility, according to official University documents, was "administrative supervision under the President over academic policy, undergraduate and graduate curriculum and the Faculty and its departments of instruction." In the next few years Brandeis also moved to adopt more traditional academic departments within the undergraduate and graduate schools.

The reorganization of the University structure necessitated the codification of a faculty tenure and promotion policy. In 1958 Dean of Faculty Saul Cohen drafted the first Brandeis Faculty Handbook, defining guidelines for academic tenure and delineating the role and responsibility of the faculty. The handbook also set up formal faculty advisory bodies: the Faculty Meeting for legislation, the Faculty Senate for representation, departments and school councils for administration, and faculty committees for counsel.

From its inception, the University had committed its resources to creating programs that would provide the best possible education of the whole person, resisting the temptation to strengthen one area at the expense of another. By the mid-1950s Brandeis had achieved distinction in the humanities and social sciences with a talented faculty that included Herbert Marcuse, John Roche, Claude Vigee, Marie Syrkin, Philip Rieff, J. V. Cunningham, Irving Howe, Robert Preyer, Maurice Stein, Jean-Pierre Barricelli, Rudolf Kayser, Denah Lida, Lawrence Fuchs, and I. Milton Sacks. To establish a high-quality research university in postwar America, further development of both faculty and facilities in the School of Science was required.

The timing was fortuitous. The growth of science and technology in the late 1940s, the establishment of the National Science Foundation in 1950, and the launch of Sputnik in 1957 – all propelled science and science education headlong into the latter part of the twentieth-century, what President Eisenhower called "the vestibule of a vast new technological age" in his 1960 State of the Union message. This was for Brandeis the brief, but significant, "window of opportunity," as it has been characterized by Saul Cohen who, as first chairman of the School of Science and first dean of faculty, played a crucial part in the University's development as a research institution.

In transforming the young school, the administration, with the assistance of a distinguished science advisory committee, including physicist Leo Szilard, was determined

The Kalman Science Building, December 18, 1956. The familiar grape arbor and wishing well remained campus landmarks until the construction of the new science complex in 1965.

not to sacrifice depth for breadth. In the sciences, as in other areas, decisions were made to pursue a large, but limited, number of disciplines: programs in biology, chemistry, physics, and mathematics were established, while concentrations in such areas as geology and geography were not. Brandeis remained committed to quality in all that it undertook, seeking strength in those areas in which it could excel. University documents of the time noted the criteria: ". . . these areas must be at once vital to our time and consistent with the thousand-year-old tradition of university education."

The early curriculum in biology, for example, focussed on laboratory aspects where application of chemistry was opening paths, but not on work in other more traditional areas where older and larger schools had pioneered. A department in theoretical physics was started in 1956; experimental physicists were not recruited for the faculty until 1961 when resources for establishing a first-rate program became available. During these years, boundaries between disciplines were beginning to blur and interdisciplinary research and teaching were emerging as exciting and innovative concepts. As an early advocate of programs of interrelated study, Brandeis demonstrated great resourcefulness in maximizing the strengths and depths of its scientific talent.

By the end of the first decade, the University had established twelve graduate programs in its four schools. As each area of study developed, a single scholar was able to attract a group of colleagues to Brandeis with the promise of academic freedom and intellectual rigor. The opportunity to create a new program or department brought a cadre of gifted academicians and innovative scientists; freedom to pursue knowledge has remained one of the strongest attractions of university teaching. Among those forming the nucleus of the first research faculty were biologist Albert Kelner, biophysicist Herman Epstein, experimental psychologists Ricardo Morant and Richard Held, and chemists Saul Cohen, Sidney Golden, and Orrie Friedman. By the late 1950s the faculty had expanded and included biochemists Nathan Kaplan and Martin Kamen, physicists David Falkoff,

Eugene Gross, Silvan Schweber, Max Chretien, and Jack Goldstein, and mathematicians Oscar Goldman, Arnold Shapiro, Maurice Auslander, and Edgar Brown.

These young scientists had already proved themselves able to secure funding for their own pursuits. The wellspring of support for basic research from both the federal government and private foundations provided a financial base for the University's earliest projects. Chairman of the National Science Board, James B. Conant, explained the philosophy underlying postwar research support in the first *Annual Report of the National Science Foundation* published in 1951: "... there is no substitute for first-class men. Ten second-rate scientists or engineers cannot do the work of one who is in the first rank." Brandeis would thrive in an atmosphere where the pursuit of excellence took precedence over institutional size or history.

Although individual scientists were able to garner significant basic support for their work, modern research requires expensive equipment and facilities. In the late 1950s, the University undertook a program of construction that has kept pace as advances in science require larger and more advanced and expensive structures.

The first major financial incentive for the construction of research facilities came in 1953 when the University was challenged to match a $500,000 grant from the Charles Hayden Foundation. Until this time, all science activities had been housed on the upper floor of Ford Hall with experimental psychology laboratories installed in one of the Ridgewood houses. Brandeis succeeded in raising the required matching funds and ground was broken for the first campus research structures. In 1956 the Kalman Science Research Center in the Hayden Science Quadrangle was completed, followed in 1958 by the Friedland Life Science Center. Individual gifts and foundation grants followed and were used to establish new programs in the sciences and to provide state-of-the-art equipment and facilities.

The success of these early endeavors and the continuing support for basic research encouraged the University to redouble its efforts. On November 8, 1965 a special science convocation marked the dedication of the Gerstenzang Science Quadrangle. The new buildings quadrupled the existing facilities for work in biochemistry, chemistry, physics, biology, and mathematics. The two-room science library in Kalman was replaced by the larger and more efficient new Gerstenzang Library. There were laboratories for work in endocrinology, photobiology, biochemical genetics, radiation chemistry, molecular physics, as well as offices, seminar rooms, photographic darkrooms, and an observatory. The new construction altered forever the face of the campus, replacing remnants of the past with modern structures of the future.

In the early 1960s, following more than a decade of unprecedented growth and accomplishment, two significant developments galvanized the Brandeis community. On August 30, 1961, following an intensive three-year study, the University was notified of authorization to establish a chapter of Phi Beta Kappa. Recognized as the highest achievement in American undergraduate education, Phi Beta Kappa designation had come in thirteen years, the shortest time since the organization's founding in the eighteenth century. In the report issued by the Committee on Qualifications of the United Chapters of Phi Beta Kappa, the reviewers commented on their investigation: "These statistics bear graphic witness to the zeal for excellence that characterizes the entire spirit of the University. They bear witness also to the University's remarkable achievement in creating in ten years' time – only three student generations – a full-fledged institution capable of providing undergraduate instruction comparable to that offered by other American universities of the first rank." On October 8, 1961, thirteen years since its inauguration, Brandeis University celebrated the founding of the Mu chapter of Phi Beta Kappa.

Equally dramatic was the announcement on April 30, 1963 of a $6 million Ford Foundation Challenge Grant to Brandeis to assist in general program development. As so many times before, the University community mobilized and before two of the three years allotted had passed, $18 million had been raised to meet the "three for one" Ford Foundation challenge. In December 1964 a second $6 million Ford Challenge Grant was announced and Brandeis responded. In a little more than three years, Brandeis had raised $48 million, gaining the confidence and respect of the academic world and moving dramatically closer to financial stability.

The Phi Beta Kappa designation and Ford Challenge grants were turning points in the University's history, fulfillment of the earliest dreams of the founders and testament to the vision of those who had seen Brandeis through a critical and successful transformation.

During the next decade, achievement followed achievement. Repeatedly, many of the University's undergraduate and graduate programs were cited among the nation's best by the American Council on Education. In 1970 the chemistry and physics departments were designated by the National Science Foundation as "centers of excellence," recipients of major Science Development Program grants established to support outstanding work and to reward institutions that demonstrated the potential for leadership.

By the early 1970s, Brandeis had also earned distinction in the physical and life sciences, gaining renown for programs in medically-related research. In 1972 a single gift established a locus for the University's medically-oriented work in biochemistry, biology, chemistry, microbiology, psychology, sociology, and social welfare. The new Rosenstiel Basic Medical Sciences Research Center centralized the activities of the University's schol-

From left, President Abram Sachar and Chairman of the Brandeis Board of Trustees Norman Rabb at press conference announcing second Ford Foundation Grant, December 20, 1964. The award of a second grant affirmed the Ford Foundation's faith in the future of Brandeis and helped secure financial stability for the University's continued growth and development.

ars and scientists and its research fellows involved in medically-related work and provided support for symposia, colloquia, and publications. Distinguished microbiologist Harlan Halvorson was named first director of the Rosenstiel and guided the Center's work for the next fifteen years. In 1975 the Henry and Lois Foster Biomedical Research Laboratories were built to provide additional facilities for Brandeis scientists engaged in basic research in biology, biochemistry, and biomedical areas.

The decision to turn a small liberal arts school into a research university had been a calculated risk. The dramatic transformation was marked by enormous changes to the landscape, rapid expansion of student enrollment, and increased promise of financial security. As President Sachar observed, "Change had become the Brandeis tradition."

*A biology class
in Ford Hall,
January 1951.
Within a decade
Brandeis would
be dramatically
transformed
into a research
institution with
state-of-the-art
laboratory and
teaching
facilities.*

Dr. Saul G. Cohen in his laboratory ca. 1954. As Chairman of the School of Science, first Chairman of the Graduate Committee in Chemistry, and first Dean of Faculty, Dr. Cohen played a major role in the transformation of Brandeis from a liberal arts school into a research university.

OPPOSITE:
At right, founding faculty member and assistant professor of chemistry, Dr. Stuart Allan Mayper, directing students in an experiment in fractional distillation, November 1950.

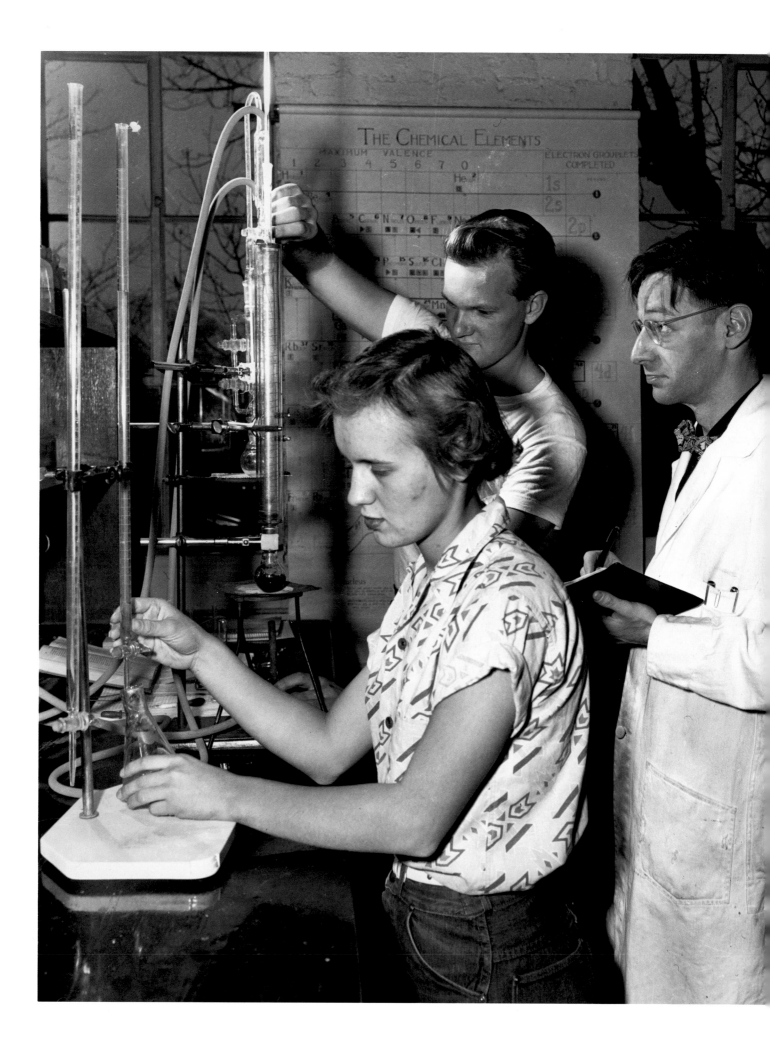

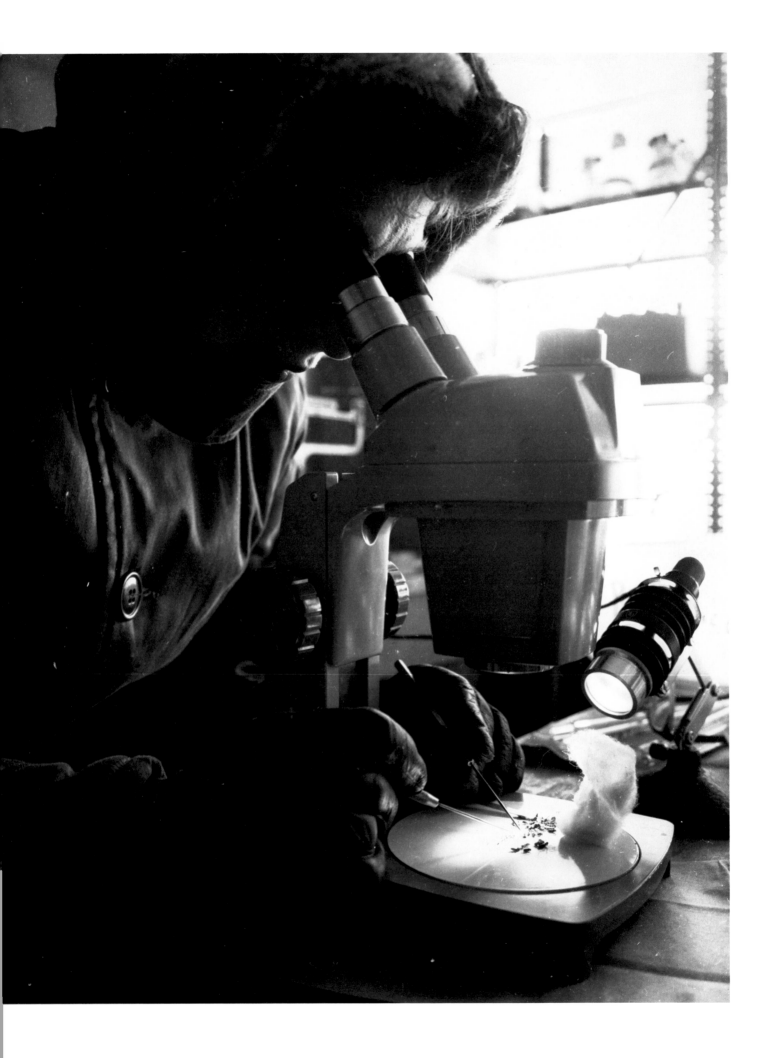

Dr. Miriam Schurin, associate professor of biology, experimenting with fruit flies in a near-freezing laboratory environment, ca. 1960.

Associate professor of biology Dr. Jerome Schiff and colleague in laboratory, ca. 1964.

"*From my initial interview with President Charles Schottland and Dr. Sidney Farber in 1970, I learned not only of the excitement of a small research university, but also of the opportunity of developing a research institute which bridged basic science departments and clinical practice. While it is unusual for such a small university to host such a large-endowed biomedical research institute, the quality of its science faculty, the strength of its undergraduate and graduate educational programs, and the commitment to pushing back the frontiers in medical science, were all consistent with the efforts of a brash, young university.*"

H. O. HALVORSON
Professor of Biology and Director, Rosenstiel Basic Medical Sciences Research Center, 1972–1987

*Science Convocation and dedication
of the Gerstenzang Science
Quadrangle, October 7, 1965.
Honorary degrees were awarded to
twelve internationally-renowned
scientists who had gathered for a
series of meetings and seminars prior
to the formal dedication ceremony.*

Honorary degree recipients at the Science Convocation, October 7, 1965. Seated left to right: Dr. Severo Ochoa, 1959 Nobel Laureate in Medicine; James E. Webb, administrator of NASA; Brandeis president Dr. Sachar; Brandeis Board of Trustees chairman Norman Rabb; Dr. Robert Burns Woodward, 1965 Nobel Laureate in Chemistry; and Dr. Albert Szent-Gyorgi, 1937 Nobel Laureate in Medicine. Standing left to right: Dr. Carl Cori, 1947 Nobel Laureate in Medicine; Gerard Piel, publisher of Scientific American; *Dr. Jerome Wiesner, Dean of the School of Science, MIT; Dr. Chaim Pekeris, Weizmann Institute of Science, Rehovoth, Israel; Dr. Torbjörn Caspersson, Nobel Institute for Medicine, Stockholm; Dr. Oscar Zariski, Robinson Professor of Mathematics, Harvard University; Dr. Ernest Nagel, John Dewey Professor of Philosophy, Columbia University; and Dr. Isidore I. Rabi, 1944 Nobel Laureate in Physics.*

New staff members assuming the many duties of Jan Gilmore, secretary of the anthropology department, fall 1964.

A Brandeis physics laboratory, August 1965. A department of theoretical physics was founded at Brandeis in 1956 followed five years later by an experimental program. In 1970 the Brandeis physics department was designated "A Center of Excellence" by the National Science Foundation and awarded a grant for further development of laboratory facilities. Today the Brandeis physics faculty of twenty-six includes experimentalists, theoretical physicists, biophysicists, and astrophysicists.

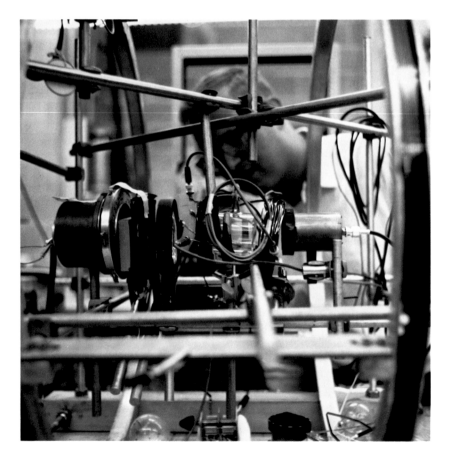

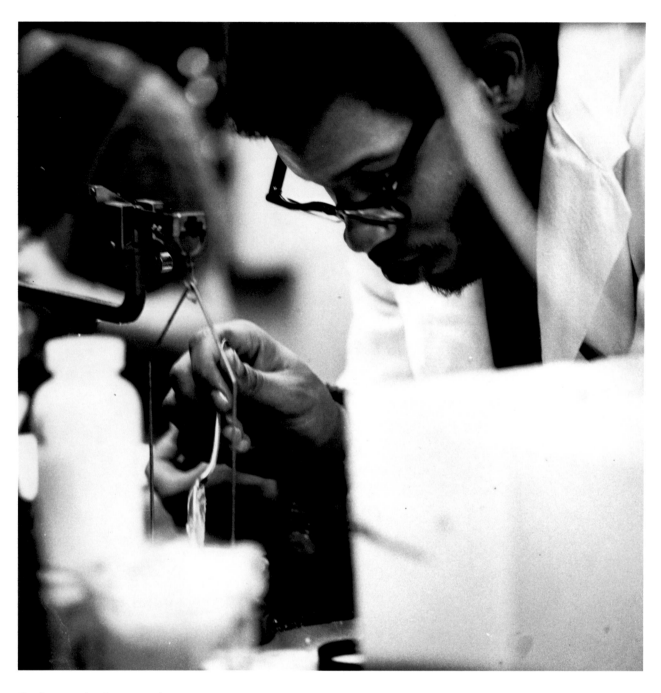

*Student conducting research
in a biochemistry laboratory,
November 1968. The Department of
Biochemistry was founded in 1957 by
Nathan Kaplan and Martin Kamen
and has been cited among the
nation's finest by the American
Council on Education for nearly
three decades. The Department of
Biochemistry now includes a faculty
of seventeen, providing extensive
opportunities for students in a broad
spectrum of research.*

The Bassine Biological Studies
Center houses the research activities
of the Department of Biology, winter
1965. The major research areas of the
seventeen-member faculty include
molecular genetics and development,
neurobiology, immunology, and cell
and structural biology.

*The Leo Gerstenzang Science
Library and Quadrangle, July 1967.
The new structures quadrupled
the University's facilities for research
and teaching in biology, chemistry,
biochemistry, microbiology, physics,
and mathematics. The new
Gerstenzang Library, supported by
the Brandeis University National
Women's Committee, replaced the
two-room facility in the Kalman
Science Building.*

"A distinguished university president once told me that no educator in his right mind would have designed Brandeis University as it has developed since 1948. Fortunately, the logic and pace of normal institutional growth were far removed from the minds of the University's founders. Who but the Brandeis founders would have created a liberal arts university with such a rich curriculum and such limited resources? Who but the Brandeis trustees, donors, and faculty aimed early on to establish almost instantaneously a research university on such a small base of staffing, student body, and financial support? Who but the Brandeis founders would have invested so heavily in music, theater, art, and a museum, in a university with an undergraduate enrollment that did not reach 1,000 until about 1960 and has not exceeded 3,000 since that time? Who but the Brandeis trustees would have initiated graduate work in the sciences with expansive and expensive requirements for outstanding scientists, able technicians, doctoral candidates, and experimental laboratories? What other university leaders would have committed the University to mount an innovative graduate program dealing with the study of social welfare policy and administration instead of following the conventional objective of building a law school bearing the name of Justice Brandeis? And only at Brandeis has a small group of women fashioned a nationwide network of supporters of the central requisite of learning and scholarship – the library, the laboratory of the mind.

"The inordinately ambitious and illogical goals embraced by the Brandeis family set the tone and hastened the pace of the University's growth. In reaching for the academic stars, Brandeis telescoped into a few years the normal development of a century in the life of a university. It was unremitting effort that enabled Brandeis to be recognized within a few years as a small, secular liberal arts research university of high quality. Those of us who labored at various stages since 1948 to reconcile lofty aims and inadequate resources have sometimes deplored the constraints that kept our goals beyond fulfillment. Yet none of us would have wanted Brandeis to be less ambitious."

MARVER H. BERNSTEIN
President, 1972–1983

*The Rosenstiel Basic Medical
Sciences Research Facilities, 1975.
The construction of the Rosenstiel
and Foster buildings in the 1970s
enabled the University's work to
expand as Brandeis became a
respected new center for basic
medical research.*

Dr. Stephan Berko, William R. Kenan, Jr. Professor of Physics, ca. 1985. Dr. Berko has been instrumental in developing the teaching and research program in experimental physics at Brandeis. The Brandeis faculty now includes eight Fellows of the National Academy of Science: Dr. Robert Abeles, Department of Biochemistry; Dr. Stuart Altman, Heller School; Dr. Berko; Dr. Martin Gibbs, Department of Biology; Dr. Ernest Grunwald, Department of Chemistry; Dr. William Jencks, Department of Biochemistry; Dr. Alfred Nisonoff, Department of Biology; and Dr. Alfred Redfield, Department of Biochemistry.

Associate professor of biophysical chemistry Judith Herzfeld, fall 1987.

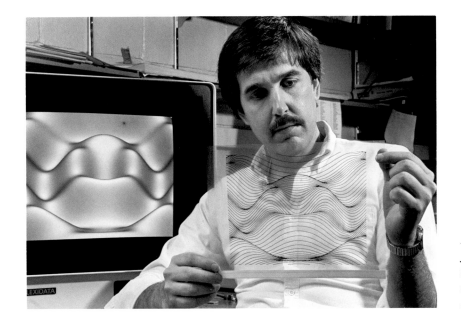

Associate professor of psychology James Todd, whose research includes the perception of form and motion, mathematical modeling, and computer graphics, 1987.

THE ARTS AND THE UNIVERSITY

"The Creative Instinct"

"... the function of the University in respect to the fine arts is not limited to promoting understanding and appreciation. It should strive to awaken the slumbering creative instinct, to encourage its exercise and development, to stimulate production."

LOUIS D. BRANDEIS
Letter to his niece Fanny Brandeis, October 1924

The University's commitment to programs of excellence also embraced the creative arts. Their inclusion in the curriculum was assured by a long and rich artistic heritage. And while it has been a struggle for the arts to gain respectability in American higher education, at Brandeis they have been neither "ugly ducklings" nor "Cinderellas," to borrow from Clark Kerr's 1963 Godkin Lectures at Harvard. The promise was made early to give a home at Brandeis to art, music, and theatre.

The School of Music, Drama and Fine Arts opened in 1949, one year later than the School of General Studies and the other "upper" divisions. Although time and resources affected the evolution of programs – advancing the growth of certain disciplines and deferring the development of others – the creative arts have always been central to the idea of a Brandeis liberal arts education.

The first courses offered by the School of Music, Drama and Fine Arts were classes in music taught by the first (and only) member of the arts faculty, Erwin Bodky. A respected musician and scholar and former student of Richard Strauss, Bodky came to Brandeis in 1949 from the Longy School of Music in Cambridge. In 1950 Bodky was joined by Irving Fine, appointed lecturer in music and composer-in-residence. Like the many creative scientists who came to Brandeis, artists such as Bodky and Fine saw an opportunity to foster and develop an innovative arts program unencumbered by generations of academic convention. A young university could experiment and take chances and there were exciting new possibilities for both faculty and students.

For the 1951–1952 term the School of Creative Arts (as it would be known henceforth) offered students concentrations in music, drama, and fine arts. Leonard Bernstein was named professor of music and director of the School whose faculty had grown to include composer Harold Shapero, lecturer in music; *Time* drama critic Louis Kronenberger, visiting lecturer in the dramatic arts; and painter Mitchell Siporin, artist-in-residence.

OPPOSITE:
A performance of The Front Page, *the classic play on the fourth estate by Ben Hecht and Charles MacArthur, March 3, 1981. The Spingold production was directed by professor of theatre arts Charles Werner Moore.*

Dr. Erwin Bodky, at piano, with colleagues, ca. 1950. The distinguished musicologist and musician and former student of Richard Strauss founded the Brandeis creative arts program in 1949.

In these early days, there were no specialized facilities for the arts: theatre classes were conducted in Ullman Amphitheatre and the basement of the Shapiro Athletic Center served as a fine arts studio. But the initial shortcomings did not dissuade an extraordinary faculty of distinguished and promising artists, critics, and historians from coming to Brandeis. Mitchell Siporin explained many years later: "There were many very attractive people teaching here and the school had the promise of being different. . . . The whole place had an air of adventure and improvisation."

As programs were developing, a group of foster alumni organized the Friends of the School of Music, later the Friends of the School of Creative Arts. During the crucial early years when activities in the arts were just beginning to take shape and there were few resources, the Friends sponsored concerts, lectures, and fund-raising events to support the University's artistic programs.

The creative arts drew the spotlight early to the young and innovative institution with the staging of the first Brandeis Festival of the Creative Arts in 1952. The festival, organized as part of the first commencement, captured the imagination of the national media. Critics and reviewers flocked to the Waltham campus to observe and review the young University's ambitious efforts.

Planned and directed by Leonard Bernstein, the festival consisted of four days of music, dance, theatre, film, and poetry, as the festival program described, "a sustained and integrated inquiry into the state of creative arts." Events included the world premiere performance of Bernstein's one-act opera, *Trouble in Tahiti* (composed for the occasion), and the premiere of Marc Blitzstein's adaptation of Kurt Weill's *The*

Three-Penny Opera in a concert version with Lotte Lenya. Performances of Stravinsky's *Les Noces* and Pierre Schaeffer's *Symphonie Pour Un Homme Seul* featured the dancing and choreography of Merce Cunningham, and Bernstein led members of the Boston Symphony Orchestra in a memorial concert for Serge Koussevitzky who had served as an advisor to the Brandeis music program. Another advisory committee member, Aaron Copland, participated as a pre-concert discussant. Festival activities also included a jazz concert and discussion, an "art" film series, and poetry readings by William Carlos Williams, Karl Shapiro, and Peter Viereck. Festival events took place on the stage of the Ullman Amphitheatre still under construction only hours before the first audience members began to arrive.

For the 1953 commencement the following June, Mr. Bernstein staged a variety of programs related to the theme of the second festival, "An Exploration of the Comic Spirit." This event, like its ambitious predecessor, encompassed both performances and discussions, including the American premiere of Poulenc's comic and controversial opera, *Les Mamelles de Tiresias*; Morton Gould's *Concerto for Tap Dancer and Orchestra* with Danny Daniels as soloist; the premiere reading of Louis Kronenberger's *The International Set* directed by Eric Bentley and starring Mildred Dunnock, Edna Best, and Mildred Natwick; and a symposium on the American comic strip with Al Capp and Milton Caniff. Mitchell Siporin organized "Three Centuries of the Comic Spirit," an exhibition of the works of Saul Steinberg and Fernand Leger and a survey of the comic in the visual arts from Tiepolo to Daumier. An evening symposium entitled "The Comic Performer" featured moderators Fred Allen and S. J. Perelman with panelists Jack Gilford, Arthur Kober, Alice Pearce, and Irwin Corey. There were also readings of comic poetry and a student performance of Pergolesi's *La Serva Padrona*.

The Creative Arts Festival continued on an irregular basis through the 1950s and the early 1960s. In 1955 composer Darius Milhaud and conductor Izler Solomon directed performances of Milhaud's opera, *Medea*, and his choral ballet, *Salade*, as well as Vallency's *The Thracian Horses*. The 1957 festival featured a jazz symposium and premieres of specially-commissioned works, modern dance presentations, poetry readings by Richard Wilbur and Robert Lowell, and exhibitions of work by Stuart Davis, Jimmy Ernst, and Max Weber.

During the 1960s, the festivals were student-sponsored, offering programs of both traditional and experimental work. The Brandeis Folk Festival began as part of these celebrations and soon became a popular annual event, drawing thousands of area college students to a variety of folk, blues, and bluegrass performances, symposia, and workshops.

The creative talent guiding the early festivals was also responsible for the design of the arts curricula. With the counsel of the Advisory Committee on Educational Policies in Music, the faculty established innovative academic programs incorporating both the scholarly study of history and theory and the active experience of the creative process.

By 1953 the strength of the music department was widely recognized. Composer Arthur Berger had joined Bodky, Fine, Bernstein, and Shapero in establishing a graduate program in composition. Master's and doctoral degree programs in music history, analysis, and criticism were added the following year, as the faculty expanded to include Kenneth Levy and Caldwell Titcomb and later, Paul Brainard and Martin Boykan.

In 1957 the Slosberg Music and Arts Center was opened, providing classrooms, practice rooms, a 250-seat recital hall, and gallery space, a much-needed first home for the arts. By this time the music department housed an electronic music studio and had become a center of contemporary composition. It was not long before the burgeoning program outgrew the space and additional offices and practice rooms were added in 1963.

In the early years, music students were offered private vocal and instrumental instruction with well-known Boston-area musicians, many of whom were members of the Boston Symphony. In 1959, Robert Koff, a founding member of the Juilliard String Quartet, joined the faculty to expand and direct student performance activities. Koff remained for more than twenty years, assembling a talented group of visiting and adjunct faculty as lecturers and instructors, and as performers with students and faculty in a busy schedule of campus musical events.

The fine arts department was likewise founded by a single faculty member, painter Mitchell Siporin, who served initially as a one-person studio and history department. Siporin had been a WPA artist in the 1930s and came to Brandeis in 1951 from the American Academy in Rome. In 1953 historian Leo Bronstein and sculptor Peter Grippe joined Siporin, tripling the fine arts faculty and expanding the number and scope of classes and activities.

The fine arts department, like its artistic siblings, was designed to be a dynamic creative program within a liberal arts curriculum. Siporin, Grippe, and Bronstein set a precedent by building a faculty of both working artists and scholars, including, in time, Sam Hunter, William Seitz, Creighton Gilbert, Arthur Polonsky, Joachim Gaede, and Gerald Bernstein. The construction of the Goldman-Schwartz Fine Arts Building in 1962 furnished new studio, office, and classroom facilities. The Pollack Fine Arts Teaching Center was added in 1972 to accommodate expanding activities.

Supplementing and enriching the fine arts program since the early days has been a "second" faculty of visiting artists under the auspices of the Ziskind Visiting Professorships, the Jack and Lillian Poses Institute for the Arts, and the Saltzman Artist-in-Residence Program. With these resources, the department has served as a temporary home for a host of important visiting scholars and artists, most notably historians Arnold Hauser and Rudolf Arnheim, painters Jacob Lawrence, Philip Guston, Frank Stella, and Elaine de Kooning, and sculptors Penelope Jencks and Stephen Antonakos.

Even before Brandeis had established a fine arts department, there was a University art collection. In 1950 a bequest of nearly 200 paintings by Boston patron of contemporary art, Louis Schapiro, established a permanent collection for the new University. Similar donations followed and the works were given their premiere public showing at the first Creative Arts Festival.

Although these early gifts showed a strong contemporary emphasis, the University's initial plans called for building a comprehensive teaching collection of work from all periods. Later, as the realities of inflated prices, scarcity of acquisitions, and financial belt-tightening diminished these hopes, the early contemporary focus developed into the strength and singularity of the Brandeis collection.

For years, Siporin and acting curator Walter Spink organized exhibitions in a variety of campus locations while the permanent University art collection was stored in temporary quarters on and off campus. Finally, in 1961, to fulfill the increasing need for

Professor Mitchell Siporin and studio art class in Shapiro Athletic Center, ca. 1950. Painter Siporin founded the Brandeis fine arts department and conducted both studio and art history classes while overseeing the early University art collection.

exhibition space and to provide a home for the permanent collection, the Edward and Bertha Rose Museum was built. Critic and curator Sam Hunter was appointed first director.

Hunter focussed his energy and interest on acquiring a broad range of contemporary work. The Gevirtz-Mnuchin Fund was established during Hunter's tenure, enabling the University to purchase twenty-one "experimental" works including important paintings by Larry Rivers, James Rosenquist, Ellsworth Kelly, Kenneth Noland, and Morris Louis. Seemingly overnight, Hunter was able to shape a distinguished modern collection with a decidedly contemporary point of view. Hunter left the University in 1965 and was succeeded by William Seitz, whose training as a painter and historian served the museum well in the continuing acquisition of modern and contemporary work. The third Rose head, Michael Wentworth, supervised the addition of a new wing to the museum in 1974 for improved office, preparation, exhibition, and storage space.

Under its current director Carl Belz, the Rose has strengthened its position as a leader in contemporary art, redefining and consolidating the collection to make the Museum a home for "the art being made around us." The permanent collection now totals 10,000 works, including the holdings of the Helen S. Slosberg Collection of Oceanic Art, the Trustman Collection of Daumier Prints, the Riverside Museum Collection, and the Tumen Collection of Jewish Ceremonial Objects.

For more than twenty-five years the Rose Museum has presented an eclectic series of exhibitions ranging from large-scale surveys of modern American and European painting and sculpture to smaller one-person shows devoted to the work of seminal figures in contemporary art such as Philip Guston, Frank Stella, Jennifer Bartlett, Hans Hofmann,

Katherine Porter, and video artist Nam June Paik. And in little more than a decade, the Lois Foster Boston-Area Artists Exhibition has become an important annual event recognized for presenting the work of emerging local painters and sculptors.

Finding its full measure somewhat more slowly, the theatre program was established in 1951 by visiting professor of dramatic art, noted critic and historian Louis Kronenberger. The department expanded during the next few years with part-time faculty and a full-time staff that came to include John Matthews, Edwin Burr Pettet, and James Clay. Student participation in all phases of theatrical productions was crucial to the early development of the program and integral to the Brandeis model of a university as a working community of scholar-teachers and student-apprentices. The Brandeis Theatre Workshop of the 1950s evolved into an intensive study of theoretical and practical problems presenting two major student productions a year, six studio productions, lectures by guests from the professional theatre, field trips to Boston performances, and additional lectures and discussions by staff. Workshop students also participated in the early Creative Arts Festivals.

The first campus theatrical performances were student productions presented by the Drama Club, the Gilbert and Sullivan Society, and the Hi Charlie Review. These were often ambitious productions, ranging from *Lysistrata* to *The Pirates of Penzance*. In 1958, after years of presenting a variety of studio productions, the theatre arts program mounted its first full-scale public performance, a production of Garcia Lorca's *The House of Bernarda Alba* directed by Edwin Burr Pettet.

The theatre program grew rapidly and by the early 1960s, a facility was needed to realize both the artistic and educational potential of theatre at the University. In 1965 the Nate and Frances Spingold Theatre complex was completed, housing a 750-seat main stage theatre; the Laurie Flexible Theatre for experimental and television productions; the Merrick Theatre, a director's space for rehearsals and student performances; and dance studios, the Dreitzer Art Gallery, and other studio, classroom, and technical workshop areas. Dedication of the Spingold highlighted the 1965 commencement devoted to "The University and the Performing Arts."

In the 1965–1966 academic year, distinguished actor Morris Carnovsky and Broadway designer Howard Bay joined the faculty to assist in the development of graduate study in theatre. In Carnovsky's first season as resident director of the acting program, the Spingold mounted productions of *Volpone*, John Arden's *The Waters of Babylon, King Lear*, and Arthur Adamov's *Ping Pong*. The following year, Bay organized a professional acting company in a theatrical season that included Chekhov's *The Seagull* directed by Carnovsky; Jules Feiffer's *Only When I Laugh* directed by James Clay; the world premiere of Don Petersen's *Does A Tiger Wear A Necktie?* directed by Charles Werner Moore; *The Tempest* starring Carnovsky; and the American premiere of John Arden's *The Workhouse Donkey*.

The inaugural Spingold seasons set the precedent for a Brandeis theatre tradition sustained and nurtured since by a dedicated faculty including Howard Bay, James Clay, Charles Werner Moore, Martin Halpern, Theodore Kazanoff, and Michael Murray, and a host of eminent visiting actors, directors, and designers.

In addition to building distinguished academic programs and maintaining an active year-round schedule of concerts, theatre performances, and art exhibitions, the University

Poses Creative Arts Awards
ceremonies in New York, April 24,
1966. On left is Meyer Schapiro,
University Professor of Fine Arts and
Archaeology at Columbia University,
recipient of the 1966 Notable
Achievement Award. This special
distinction was established in
1964 to honor those "whose
accomplishments so transcend the
normal categories that special
recognition is due."

also had an early interest in expanding the Brandeis commitment and influence in the creative arts beyond the campus. In 1956, as part of the celebration of the Justice Brandeis Centennial, the Brandeis Creative Arts Awards were established "as an expression of the University's conviction that educational institutions should play an important role in the encouragement and development of the artistic and cultural life of America." With juries as distinguished as the award winners and chaired through the years by David Wodlinger, Louis Kronenberger, Dore Schary, Harold Clurman, and Edward Albee, the Creative Arts Awards have enabled Brandeis to be both advocate and patron of the arts.

The Poses Creative Arts Awards of Brandeis University are currently given in four major categories: Fine Arts; Literature; Music and Dance; and Theatre Arts, Film, and Photography. Medals are bestowed on "established artists in celebration of a lifetime of distinguished achievement"; citations are awarded to "particularly talented artists in the same fields who are in earlier stages of their careers or who may not yet have won a similar degree of public recognition." Special commission awards for notable achievement in the creative arts were inaugurated in 1964 to honor those "whose accomplishments so transcend the normal categories that special recognition is due." Recipients of the Notable Achievement Awards include R. Buckminster Fuller, Meyer Schapiro, Alfred Barr, Jr., Isaac Stern, Lewis Mumford, Edwin Denby, John Cage, George Balanchine, and Rudolf Serkin.

The founding of Brandeis coincides with the contemporary period in the creative arts, an era of enormous change and rapid growth. Carl Belz noted the striking coincidence in his introductory essay to the twenty-fifth anniversary publication of the Rose Art Museum by drawing a parallel between the University art collection and the history of the University itself, observing how each "embodied a spirit of innovation, experimentation, and risk – a spirit that embraced change rather than the status quo."

OPPOSITE:
A summer concert, 1962. Music has remained an important campus activity for four decades with year-round series of concerts featuring faculty, students, guest artists, and since 1980, Brandeis quartet-in-residence, the Lydian String Quartet.

ABOVE:
Brandeis composer-in-residence and professor of music, Irving Fine, at piano, February 25, 1951. With faculty members Harold Shapero, Leonard Bernstein, and Arthur Berger, Fine helped establish a program in music composition and an important new center of American music.

"I most vividly remember my first interview with Arthur Berger in that small white house which served as an administration building. The graduate program in music had only recently begun and, as a prospective student, I felt the surge of optimism not only for my future, but for the future of contemporary music. The Brandeis music department seemed not merely to support innovation in music, but to be at its very center."

ALVIN LUCIER, M.F.A. '60

Modern dance in B100 in the Castle,
January 1951. At various times, B100
served as a snack bar, gymnasium,
classroom, dance studio, and theatre
rehearsal space.

Comedian Jimmy Durante and Prom
Queen Gail Leonard '56, March 7,
1953.

The Hi Charlie Review performed in the Castle, April 14, 1951. The popular satire of Brandeis life was written, composed, directed, acted, and performed by students.

"I spent my life in Ullman Amphitheatre, either as a dancer or as an actress or as a stagehand. It was the whole world for me and made the time at school a creative experience, one that prepared me for the kind of profession in which I wished to participate. When I was a senior, Brandeis permitted me the possibility of discovering my voice as a creative artist. They encouraged me to have a whole evening of my own dance works. It was a massive effort and one that now all of my students who wish a professional career must accomplish. Thanks to Brandeis for taking a chance on my talents."

GIGI CHAZIN-BENNAHUM '58

*Leonard Bernstein and members of
the Boston Symphony Orchestra in
rehearsal for the world premiere
performance of his opera,* Trouble in
Tahiti, *for the first Brandeis Creative
Arts Festival, June 12, 1952. At right
in photograph, workmen complete
construction of seating for Ullman
Amphitheatre.*

OPPOSITE:
Maestro Bernstein rehearsing
Trouble in Tahiti, *directed by Elliot
Silverstein, sets and costumes by
Ariel Baliff, June 1952.*

Igor Stravinsky's choral ballet,
Les Noces, *was featured at the
first Brandeis Festival of the
Creative Arts, June 14, 1952, with
choreography by Merce Cunningham
performed by the Cunningham
Dance Group.*

OPPOSITE:
*Dancer-choreographer Danny
Daniels in* Concerto for Tap
Dancer and Orchestra *by
Morton Gould, performed at
the second Brandeis Festival of the
Creative Arts, June 13–14, 1953.
Accompanying Daniels were
members of the Boston Symphony
Orchestra and the Boston Pops
conducted by Leonard Bernstein.*

The Brandeis cast of Gilbert and Sullivan's The Pirates of Penzance *posed for photographs on the U.S.S. Constitution, ca. 1957. The Gilbert and Sullivan Society remains one of the University's oldest and most popular campus activities.*

Composer Aaron Copland during his campus visit to deliver the Adolph Ullman Memorial Lecture, April 27, 1961. Copland was a member of the Department of Music Advisory Committee in Educational Policies in the early 1950s and returned as guest lecturer on many occasions. He was awarded an honorary degree in 1957.

Louise Nevelson directing the installation of a retrospective of her work in the Rose Art Museum, May 21, 1967. Nevelson received an honorary degree from Brandeis in 1985.

Author James Baldwin addressed "The Problem of Evil in American Literature," as guest lecturer in the Adolph Ullman Memorial Lecture Series in the Creative Arts, October 24, 1962.

Novelist and critic John Updike visited Gen Ed S in May 1966. In recognition of his many contributions to American letters, Updike was awarded the Poses Creative Arts Medal for Fiction and an honorary doctor of humane letters degree by the University in 1988.

*Actor Morris Carnovsky as King
Lear in the second production of the
Spingold Theatre's inaugural season,
March 9, 1967. Carnovsky directed
University acting activities and
established the graduate program in
theatre arts with designer Howard
Bay.*

Professor of fine arts Leo Bronstein received the University's excellence in teaching award upon his retirement in May 1967 and inaugurated the celebration of Bronstein Day, now an annual Brandeis rite of spring.

Associate professor of theatre arts John F. Matthews joined the School of Creative Arts faculty in 1955. An informal moment, May 1963.

Moliere's last play, The Imaginary Invalid, *May 7, 1978, directed by theatre faculty member Daniel Gidron.*

OPPOSITE:
Spingold production of Edna Ferber's Showboat *with music by Jerome Kern and Oscar Hammerstein, December 2, 1980. Production was directed and designed by professor of theatre arts Howard Bay.*

The 1970 student production of Gilbert and Sullivan's The Mikado. *The same opera inaugurated the Gilbert and Sullivan Society's premiere season on April 4, 1952.*

A view above the Mildred S. Lee Gallery in the Rose Art Museum, ca. 1978. The Patrons and Friends of the Rose Art Museum, chaired by Mrs. Lois Foster, was established in 1977 to support an annual exhibition highlighting the work of a major contemporary artist. Patrons and Friends exhibitions have featured the work of Helen Frankenthaler, Alex Katz, Frank Stella, Katherine Porter, and Stephen Antonakos.

OPPOSITE:
The Goldman-Schwartz art studios, December 1987. Prior to the construction of the Goldman-Schwartz Fine Arts Building in 1962, studio art classes were conducted in the basement of the Shapiro Athletic Center. The new building provided modern studio, office, and classroom space for the University's expanding fine arts activities.

AN INTERNATIONAL PERSPECTIVE

"The Basis of Understanding"

"America is the land of the American University, a creation as varied and unstandardized as the country itself. At its best it is a collection of possibilities, a medley of experiences. I was, and still am, awed by the opportunities for exploring varied fields of learning here at Brandeis. Stand at the top of the steps of Shiffman. Pick a department, pick a future. . . ."

LARS FREDEN
Wien Scholar, 1971–1973

Early in its history Brandeis established ties with an international educational community. Representatives of twenty foreign universities attended the Brandeis inaugural ceremonies in 1948; the following year the first campus convocation honored United Nations ambassadors Dr. Ralph Bunche and Abba Eban. In 1951 Israeli prime minister David Ben-Gurion visited the Brandeis campus for a special student convocation, returning in 1960 and again in 1967. Trustee Eleanor Roosevelt brought her interest and involvement in world peace and international relations to her Brandeis classes and lectures and filmed her "Prospects of Mankind" television series at the University. And the Brandeis faculty has long been active in international programs through fellowships, research grants, and service as advisors and experts to educational, social, and scientific programs around the world.

For nearly forty years, Brandeis has dedicated commencements and convocations to the themes of international education and science and world peace, conferring honorary degrees on outstanding figures in philosophy, science, politics, education, and the arts, including Madame Pandit, Lord Beveridge, Marc Chagall, Pierre Mendes-France, Gunnar Myrdal, Alva Myrdal, Jean Piaget, Sir Isaiah Berlin, Torbjörn Caspersson, Jaime Cardinal Sin, Sir Ernst Gombrich, Hastings Banda, and Helen Suzman.

As early as 1953 the Brandeis student body included twenty foreign students from a dozen lands. But the involvement in international education assumed much greater significance when Brandeis became home to one of the nation's largest privately-endowed foreign student programs.

The Wien International Scholarship Program, or WISP, was founded in 1958 to accomplish three main goals: to further international understanding through education; to provide foreign students with an opportunity to study in the United States; and to enrich the intellectual and cultural life of the Brandeis community.

OPPOSITE:
Wien students at welcoming tea, ca. 1970. Now three decades old, the Wien Program has provided educational opportunities for nearly 700 students from 100 lands.

From its inception, WISP was envisioned as more than a mechanism for educating international students in America. WISP is committed to providing exceptionally gifted young people from all over the world an American college experience. In a sense, WISP has been devoted to educating future generations of international leaders in government, business, the arts, and science. Today the WISP alumni count professors in universities and schools all over the world, research scientists, diplomats, physicians, journalists, artists, and representatives to international organizations including the United Nations.

Initially, candidates for WISP were referred by the Institute of International Education; Brandeis faculty and administration contacts throughout the world also assisted in these early recruitment efforts. In time, however, as the WISP reputation for quality in international education became more widely known, embassies, consulates, schools, government agencies, and individuals created a global network of information and referral for Brandeis. And the Wien scholars themselves now serve as an international consular corps carrying the Brandeis name around the world.

On Columbus Day, October 12, 1958, the Wien Program was dedicated in ceremonies in the science quadrangle. Honorary degrees were conferred on Massachusetts senators Leverett Saltonstall and John F. Kennedy and former ambassador to the Soviet Union George F. Kennan, who delivered the convocation address. Kennan's remarks to the first Wien class reflected his own and the country's deep concern for the image of America and her people in the era of "the ugly American." In his remarks Kennan appealed to the first Wien scholars to seek in their American experience ". . . that tolerance that is the basis of all real international understanding."

In three decades, WISP has hosted 700 scholars from 100 countries. And despite prevailing trends in education and the mutability of government support, the WISP goals and achievements have remained constant to the founding commitment. The lives and futures of Wien scholars continue to be changed by their experience in America just as their presence has had a lasting and incalculable effect on the fabric of University life, providing, in the words of Brandeis president Marver Bernstein, both "an opportunity and a challenge."

The University's dedication to offering an American educational experience to an international student body was balanced by an equal concern for enabling Brandeis students to broaden their educational horizons. In the 1950s Brandeis began to participate in existing programs of study abroad such as those sponsored by Sweet Briar and Smith College.

The University assumed a leading role in foreign study for American students in 1961 when, under the direction of Dr. Howard Sachar and with the support of Frances and Jacob Hiatt, the Hiatt Institute in Israel was established. Organized as a "traveling university" with the State of Israel as its campus, the Hiatt Institute differed from other study-abroad programs of the time by not being affiliated with a specific foreign university. Instead, Brandeis faculty members and Israeli educators traveled throughout the land with Hiatt students linking lectures and discussions with field experience. The program placed emphasis on the study of contemporary Israel as well as on work in the more traditional areas of archaeology, literature, and history. Indeed, the land of Israel became the labo-

Massachusetts senator John F. Kennedy adding finishing touches to his speech for the Wien International Scholarship Program inaugural ceremony, October 12, 1958. Receiving an honorary degree along with Kennedy were Massachusetts senator Leverett Saltonstall and former United States ambassador to the Soviet Union, George F. Kennan. To the future president's left is Brandeis professor of politics John Roche.

ratory for the "Hiatts" as seminars with Israeli political and government leaders and archaeological digs and expeditions were organized to supplement classroom study.

The Hiatt Institute opened in 1961 as a summer program with thirteen Brandeis students and three Hiatt traveling faculty, Dr. Howard Sachar, Dr. Benjamin Halpern of Brandeis, and visiting professor Dr. Nadav Halevi of Hebrew University. That fall it expanded into a full semester residency for Brandeis juniors. The following year the Hiatt evolved into a national program, offering study in Israel to interested and qualified juniors from any accredited American university or college. Later it included both a fall and a spring semester.

In addition to classes and field trips, the Hiatt Institute offered internships and opportunities for volunteer work. During the 1967 and 1973 conflicts, when the participation of the Hiatt's Israeli staff in wartime service interrupted regular classes, many civilian jobs were undertaken by Hiatt students who were given the option to return home but chose, for the most part, to stay. Over the years, new courses were added to the curriculum and a permanent base of operations, Hiatt House, was established in Jerusalem.

By the mid-1960s, Hebrew University had introduced a curriculum for foreign students resembling that offered by the Hiatt. Other American and Israeli universities and civic and religious groups followed with programs of their own, many conceived on the Hiatt model. Because of the proliferation of such opportunities, the Brandeis program was

The Hiatt House in Jerusalem, ca. 1975. More than 600 students from 150 American colleges and universities participated in the Hiatt Institute in Israel between 1961 and 1983.

closed in 1983. In its twenty-two years, the Hiatt Institute had made it possible for more than 600 students from 150 colleges and universities to study in Israel.

There are now more than 100 programs of study in twenty-five foreign countries available to Brandeis students, including many in the State of Israel. The University sponsors several international scholarships including the Sachar International Fellowships which provide assistance for junior study abroad, senior thesis work, and graduate research.

The Hiatt Institute has been one of many important ties between Brandeis and the State of Israel, a relationship that has grown and flourished for forty years. From their founding in 1948, America's first Jewish-sponsored nonsectarian university and the Jewish homeland have shared a brief history and a long heritage. Indeed, for many years, Americans have been leaders in efforts to create and sustain the State of Israel. One of the early supporters was Louis Brandeis.

To celebrate this long-standing and vital relationship, Brandeis has dedicated academic convocations to Israel's leaders, awarding honorary degrees to prime ministers David Ben-Gurion (1960) and Golda Meir (1973) and to presidents Ephraim Katzir (1975) and Chaim Herzog (1987). Other Israeli political leaders as well as artists, scientists, and educators have been invited to Brandeis as guest lecturers and visiting professors and as recipients of honorary degrees. But the bonds between the University and Israel are more than ceremonial. In numerous academic exchanges and partnerships in science, social work, and communal studies, the ties uniting Brandeis and Israel have been deepened and strengthened.

The most enduring association with Israel is through the Brandeis Department of Near Eastern and Judaic Studies maintained through affiliations with leading scholars of Judaica and Israeli studies since 1948. The legacy of scholarship founded by Brandeis professors Nahum Glatzer, Simon Rawidowicz, Alexander Altmann, and Benjamin Halpern, has been nurtured and expanded through the years and the Brandeis program in Near Eastern and Judaic Studies is now the largest and most comprehensive of any in a secular university outside Israel. Nearly all graduate students in NEJS spend at least one year at a university in Israel. The Department is frequent host to visiting scholars and lecturers, and members of the Brandeis faculty teach at Israeli universities and institutes.

In 1966 the Lown School of Near Eastern and Judaic Studies was established and now serves as administrative home of the Department of Near Eastern and Judaic Studies, the Benjamin S. Hornstein Program in Jewish Communal Service, and the Maurice and Marilyn Cohen Center for Modern Jewish Studies.

The Hornstein Program in Jewish Communal Service is the only graduate program at a secular university preparing people for professional careers in the Jewish community. Since its establishment in 1969, the Hornstein program has attracted students from Israel and from other Jewish communities throughout the world. Alumni of the Hornstein program hold prominent positions in a variety of organizations in North America and Israel, as well as in Europe, Latin America, and South Africa.

The Cohen Center for Modern Jewish Studies is devoted to the study of contemporary American Jewry and functions as both a scientific research institute and a resource center for the agencies and organizations serving the needs of the American Jewish community. Applying standards long associated with Jewish scholarship to the study of the modern Jewish community, the Center also combines its scholarly work with a continuing concern for the practical implications of its research findings.

Brandeis is also home to the Tauber Institute for the Study of European Jewry, a multidisciplinary program whose special interest is exploring the causes, nature, and consequences of the European Jewish catastrophe within the context of modern European diplomatic, intellectual, political, and social history. Israeli scholars have served in various visiting capacities at the Tauber Institute, studying and lecturing on topics related to the Tauber mission.

Although the primary relationship between Brandeis and Israel is through the variety of programs devoted to Jewish studies, virtually every University department has hosted Israeli students and professors and participated in programs of academic cooperation. For nearly forty years, for example, the Brandeis Department of Chemistry has sponsored exchanges and seminars with sister institutions in Israel. As guests of Israeli universities, Brandeis scientists have helped establish and supervise research efforts in Israel. Members of the Brandeis scientific community maintain ties through educational exchanges, joint research projects, and through succeeding generations of Israeli graduate and postdoctoral students who come to study in the Brandeis School of Science.

Similarly, Israeli students of social welfare enroll in the programs of the Florence Heller Graduate School for Advanced Studies in Social Welfare and many graduates have attained prominent positions in Israeli governmental and social agencies. Through its research activities, the Heller School has also been involved in several collaborative projects with the State of Israel focussing on issues in social welfare such as housing, health care, and aging. And members of the Heller faculty and research staff are frequently invited to serve on commissions established by Israel to deal with a variety of social concerns.

For decades Brandeis has committed its resources and energies to programs of international exchange and cooperation. The need for supporting such efforts will continue to grow and evolve as global interdependence becomes reality.

*First United States ambassador to
Israel James G. McDonald and
Brandeis students outside the Castle,
March 21, 1951.*

PAGES 118-119:
*Trustee Eleanor Roosevelt addressing
the Brandeis Chapter of the United
Nations Collegiate Council in the
Castle Commons Room, ca. 1949.
In the 1960s, Mrs. Roosevelt was
visiting professor in international
relations and conducted a class
entitled, "Politics 175C: The United
Nations."*

Former French premier Pierre Mendes-France presented the 1959 commencement address and was awarded an honorary doctor of laws degree by the University, June 1959.

Madame Indira Gandhi was India's Minister of Information and Broadcasting when she delivered a Gen Ed S lecture on "The Nehru Era in India," February 4, 1965.

*Brandeis registrar and director
of admissions C. Ruggles Smith,
assisting Korean student, ca. 1953.
The Brandeis student body at this
time included twenty foreign
students.*

The first Wien scholars, May 7, 1959. The Wien International Scholarship Program was established by Lawrence and Mae Wien in October 1958 and is one of the nation's largest privately-endowed international scholarship programs.

Members of the first Wien class relaxing at Schwartz Hall, 1958.

Trustee Lawrence Wien and WISP
students from Sweden, Nigeria,
Norway, and India, October 1960.

Hiatt students on an archaeological field trip, ca. 1975. The Hiatt Institute sponsored archaeological digs and expeditions, seminars with contemporary Israeli leaders, and a variety of tours to supplement traditional classroom study.

OPPOSITE:
Hiatt students surveying a map of Israel, May 1966. The Hiatt Institute was established in 1961 by Jacob and Frances Hiatt as "a traveling University" with the State of Israel as its campus. Mr. Hiatt was Chairman of the Brandeis Board of Trustees from 1971 until 1977.

*Prime Minister Golda Meir of
Israel receiving a painting by Israeli
artist David Shariv from the fourth
president of Brandeis, Dr. Marver
Bernstein. Mrs. Meir was awarded an
honorary doctor of laws degree at a
special convocation marking the
twenty-fifth anniversaries of the
University and the State of Israel,
March 6, 1973. During the 1970s, the
University encouraged support of
the State of Israel by the American
Jewish community.*

OPPOSITE:
*Israeli prime minister David
Ben-Gurion preparing to receive an
honorary Brandeis degree, March 9,
1960. Ben-Gurion had first visited
the Brandeis campus in 1951 as the
special guest at a student-sponsored
convocation and returned in 1976 to
tape a series of historical interviews.*

*President Chaim Herzog of Israel
and Brandeis president Evelyn
Handler in academic robes,
November 15, 1987. President
Herzog received an honorary
doctor of laws degree at a special
convocation in his honor, marking
nearly four decades of cooperation
between the University and the State
of Israel.*

Interior of the Sachar International Center, ca. 1973. The Center was dedicated in April 1973 in honor of Brandeis president Abram L. Sachar and his wife, Thelma. Sited on the southwestern part of the campus, the Center provides offices, classrooms, lecture halls, and a library for many of the University's international programs and activities.

OPPOSITE:
The Sachar International Center, 1987. The Sachar Center is home to the University's two newest international programs, the Lemberg Program in International Economics and Finance and the Center for International and Comparative Studies, as well as the Department of Economics and the Gordon Public Policy Center.

"The best by-products from my decades of teaching at Brandeis are close and enduring relations with students. Solidarity naturally transplants from the classroom into the wider world. The trust endures, and as the years go by, we become friends, and stand by each other in unexpected ways and places. I wish I could name all of my former students with whom I keep in touch — those with whom I fight hunger in poor Third World countries; exchange pointers at the United Nations; cross paths in Washington; who guide my steps in Addis Ababa . . . ."

RUTH S. MORGENTHAU
Adlai E. Stevenson Professor of International Politics

SOCIAL RESPONSIBILITY & SERVICE

"The University of Conscience"

"... rights are not won on paper. They are won only by those who make their voices heard – by activists and militants. Silence never won rights. They are not handed down from above; they are forced by pressures from below. ..."

ROGER BALDWIN
Founder and Executive Director, American Civil Liberties Union, Brandeis University Commencement Address, June 8, 1969

The principles of social responsibility and service are fundamental to Brandeis, a university founded on long traditions of social justice and named for the American jurist whose work in the public interest earned his reputation as "the people's attorney."

Standards of nonsectarianism and nondiscrimination were articulated in the first press releases and publicity materials disseminated by the newly-founded University. With the establishment of admissions guidelines, it was a matter of public record that only criteria of academic talent and achievement would be used in selecting Brandeis students and that there would be no determination of enrollment based on racial, ethnic, or religious quotas. An article in the February 1952 issue of *Ebony* magazine, noted: "America's newest university... operates on a set of democratic principles which could easily serve as goals for every other university in the United States. There are no quotas limiting students of any religion and no racial barriers at Brandeis University."

Guided by these founding precepts, Brandeis has fostered an environment open to intellectual inquiry and debate. Inside the classroom and out, the dedication to freedom of expression has been evident from the beginning. In the early years, to ensure students access to ideas beyond those offered by a small faculty and limited resources, guest lecture series and visiting professorships were organized to provide a forum for the exploration of a wide spectrum of philosophical, educational, and political points of view. The commitment to openness has been sustained over the years with the University's dramatic growth and development and continued diversification of faculty and students.

Since 1956 a provocative and effective means of presenting a broad range of experience and philosophy to the University community has been through the ongoing activities of the Helmsley series. Organized "to reduce the barriers that separate races, creeds, and nationalities," the Helmsley series invite speakers from the fields of med-

OPPOSITE:
Helmsley Dialogue Series guest speaker, Dr. Martin Luther King, Jr., during his first campus visit, April 12, 1957. Dr. King had gained national attention as the leader of the Montgomery bus boycott and spoke to his Brandeis audience on "Justice Without Violence."

Civil rights leaders Roy Wilkins and Ralph Abernathy, February 29, 1957. Both Wilkins and Abernathy visited Brandeis as Helmsley Series guest speakers.

icine, education, religion, politics, labor, business, sociology, and science to address themes ranging from religious history to post-Freudian psychology to civil rights. The famous and the comparatively unknown, the widely respected and the widely controversial, Helmsley guest speakers have included Dr. Martin Luther King, Jr., Myrlie Evers, Robert Coles, B. F. Skinner, Roy Wilkins, Morris Milgram, Rollo May, Ralph Abernathy, Perry Miller, Andrew Young, Charles Silberman, William Sloane Coffin, James Gavin, and Kenneth B. Clark.

Encouraged by the University's uncompromising commitment to freedom of expression, Brandeis students have made political and social activism an important aspect of campus life. Chapters of the Students for Democratic Action and the NAACP were established in the early 1950s. Student protest focussed on a variety of traditional campus concerns, but also on larger issues of social justice and human rights. Petitions and campus demonstrations against apartheid were widespread. In the 1960s, Brandeis faculty and students sat in for Selma and marched in Montgomery.

It was fitting, therefore, that in 1959 the first professional school established at Brandeis was the Florence Heller Graduate School for Advanced Studies in Social Welfare. Since its founding, the mission of the Heller School has been to help guide American society toward bold visions of opportunity in such areas as health care, employment, and the human services. To avoid duplication of basic training that other schools of social work provide, the planners of the Heller School decided to concentrate on preparing students for senior administrative, planning, research, and teaching positions in the social welfare field. Moreover, the program was designed to recruit students who already had professional field experience or equivalent training with a faculty of both respected academics and practitioners devoting equal attention to research and training.

The first home of the Heller School was Woodruff Hall, formerly University Hall, the earliest Brandeis administration building. Charles I. Schottland, a member of the Heller School Advisory Committee, resigned as United States Commissioner of Social Security to become the first Heller dean.

In September 1959 the Heller School enrolled its pioneer class of seventeen students who brought to the new program diverse backgrounds in education, social work, and theology. In addition to Dean Schottland, the founding faculty included David French and Robert Morris. Guest lecturers were invited on a regular basis to expand the early curriculum offerings.

The Heller School began small, establishing standards and earning a reputation for excellence before broadening its curriculum and expanding faculty to number many prominent members of the social welfare community – Morris Schwartz, Robert Binstock, Howard Freeman, Herbert Apteker, Roland Warren, Gunnar Dybwad, and future Heller dean, Arnold Gurin. During the 1966–1967 school year, the School moved to its new home on a hill behind the Brandeis libraries.

From the start the unique mission and innovative approach to social problems offered by the Heller School attracted funding from government and private organizations for a variety of research and education projects. In 1960 the Ford Foundation awarded the School a major subsidy for nationwide studies on the problems of the aged. Other grants from foundations and agencies followed. More recent funding provides for research on such contemporary issues as urban public hospitals and patterns in mental health care. The Heller School has also been designated as one of the national centers assisting the government in developing policies related to health care, including important issues related to Medicare and Medicaid.

The Heller School graduated its first class in June 1961 and to date has granted nearly 500 doctorates. A master's curriculum in human services management was added in 1977, combining in one program training usually found in schools of business and public administration with those of social welfare. Since 1977 almost 300 master's degrees have been conferred. Today Heller graduates assume a variety of roles in the creation and implementation of American social welfare policy on the local, regional, and national level.

For nearly thirty years, the Heller School has been recognized for the singularity of its program in training policy makers and its continuing ability to respond to new issues, emerging social and economic realities, and political opportunities and constraints. The goal of students and faculty is to participate in the real world of social welfare policy and today the School is organized around substantive areas of concentration and supporting research, including: the Policy Center on Aging, the Bigel Institute for Health Policy, the Center for Human Resources, the Center for Social Change Practice and Theory, the Program on Labor in China, the Program on Families and Children, the Starr Center on Mental Retardation and Developmental Disabilities, and the National Institute for Sentencing Alternatives.

As Dean Stuart Altman observed at the School's twenty-fifth anniversary celebration in 1984: "Virtually every American is touched by the questions our faculty and students address."

The work of the Heller School and other University programs helped to forge an important role for Brandeis during the 1960s in a major national effort aimed at solving the complex and pressing needs of American society. Following the assassination of President Kennedy in November 1963, Brandeis received a grant to conduct scholarly research on violence. The University used the funds to sponsor three institutes on campus in December 1964, April 1965, and July 1965. At the third meeting it was recommended that a permanent research center be established and in the fall of 1965 the Center on the Study of Violence was founded. The following year psychiatrist Dr. John Spiegel was appointed to direct the program which gained national recognition as the Lemberg Center on the Study of Violence.

For nearly a decade, the work of the Lemberg Center and its staff concentrated on conducting research on the causes and consequences of violent behavior; on transmitting and applying findings through publication and consultation; and on training researchers in methods of studying violence. The results of research at the Lemberg Center were used in the formulation of national policy to understand and respond to civil unrest.

The Brandeis community and the nation were galvanized during these years by events that would profoundly affect a generation – the assassinations of Dr. Martin Luther King, Jr. and Robert Kennedy, the shooting of students at Kent State, and the escalation of the war in southeast Asia.

Dr. King visited the Brandeis campus as a Helmsley speaker in 1956 and again in 1963, addressing the themes of interracial justice and nonviolence. Following his death on April 4, 1968, the University, like the nation itself, was called on to address racism in all its forms and to search for new ways to incorporate minority interests more effectively in the life of the institution. Proposals made to the administration following the King assassination included the formation of African and Afro-American Studies departments; increased recruitment of minority faculty, students and staff; designation of scholarships in honor of Dr. King and his work; and the establishment of new programs to facilitate access to college by disadvantaged young men and women.

These issues were significant concerns for the second president of Brandeis, Morris B. Abram, who was inaugurated on October 6, 1968, and for his successor, Charles I. Schottland, who left the deanship of the Heller School to assume the University presidency in March 1970. During this period, Brandeis, like many other socially-conscious American colleges and universities, became increasingly involved in activities related to civil rights, academic reform, and the Vietnam War.

These were turbulent years for academia as college campuses became the stages for demonstrations related to a growing international wave of protest. In December 1968 Brandeis joined the national sanctuary movement giving refuge to an AWOL soldier in Mailman Hall for two weeks until his peaceful surrender to authorities.

On the afternoon of January 8, 1969, after an evening of discussion and debate of the strike at San Francisco State University, members of the Brandeis Afro-American Organization occupied Ford Hall. Ten demands were presented to President Abram and the administration, restating the proposals first presented in April following the death of Dr. King. The Ford Hall takeover lasted eleven days without violence, but the event has had lasting influence on the University.

The causes and effects symbolized by the Ford Hall events have been studied and addressed by the entire Brandeis community – administration, trustees, faculty, and students. Today the University offers a multidisciplinary concentration in the Department of African and Afro-American Studies in the School of Social Science. To honor and further the work of Dr. King, Brandeis awards annual Martin Luther King Scholarships to students who combine outstanding academic work and exceptional service to their communities.

*A sit-in of the Brandeis
administration building in
support of the student takeover
of Ford Hall, January 1969.*

Since 1968, the Transitional Year Program has provided postsecondary educational opportunities for improving basic academic skills to more than twenty-five disadvantaged young men and women each year. Students accepted in the Transitional Year Program participate in an intensive curriculum that assists in their entrance into higher education. Those who are successful in the program are encouraged and helped in their application for admission to Brandeis or to any other college or university of their choice. Nearly half of the students who complete TYP matriculate at Brandeis.

Events of national and international consequence continued to be played out on college campuses around the world as the 1960s gave way to a new decade. Reactions to the May 4, 1970 shooting of students at Kent State University and the incursion of American troops into Cambodia ignited a new national wave of student protest. Following a large rally in New Haven the National Strike Information Center was set up on the Brandeis campus to serve as a clearinghouse for information on national student political activity. The Center closed later that summer when the administration declined the continued use of campus facilities. The involvement soon after of former NSIC members in an unfortunate and tragic incident, deeply affected the Brandeis community and turned political and social activism outward to a growing national peace movement.

The intellectual strength of the Brandeis community was profoundly tested throughout this period of national dissent, for despite the potential for paralysis and disruption, the academy continued to function. In the end, the discipline of learning provided stability for a politically active and concerned campus. Brandeis had passed through the fire of the time and emerged stronger and better prepared to educate students for a world that had grown increasingly complex and divided.

Though styles of activism are transformed and reinterpreted by each new student generation, a commitment to social justice at Brandeis has endured. In 1966, during a time of great unrest, a group of students, with the assistance of chaplain Rabbi Albert Axelrad, founded the Waltham Group, an organization devoted to the betterment of the local community. For more than two decades students in the Waltham Group have given thousands of volunteer hours to a variety of programs serving the needs of the people of the City of Waltham.

Senator John Glenn discussing nuclear arms proliferation as Martin Weiner Distinguished Lecturer, October 24, 1981. Glenn returned as a presidential hopeful in 1984 to address the Brandeis Forum Series.

BELOW:
The office of the Waltham Group, 1969. Founded in 1966, the Waltham Group has been dedicated to serving the needs of the people of the City of Waltham through programs devoted to children, the elderly, and the homeless. Annually, more than 300 Brandeis students volunteer nearly 12,000 hours to a variety of community projects.

138

Annually, more than 300 Brandeis students dedicate nearly 12,000 hours to projects in the community ranging from child care and tutoring to companionship for the elderly and fund raising for the homeless. Children have been a special concern of the Waltham Group from the start. Two of the earliest and longest-running activities are an after-school program and a toddler playgroup.

The Waltham Group maintains a flexible organizational structure, adjusting activities to respond to evolving community needs. A lead poison testing program was eliminated when the state mandated testing by elementary schools and work has expanded recently to embrace new responsibility for the problems of the aged and the homeless.

Raising funds for most of its operating expenses, the Waltham Group solicits grants and donations from corporations and foundations, religious and civic groups, and friends. With hard work and ingenuity it raises a great proportion of its revenues during the annual Charity Week, particularly from the proceeds of the popular and successful Charity Auction.

At Brandeis the process of challenge and dissent in favor of fundamental human rights has united students, faculty, administration, and trustees in a common cause. Although each group follows its own course toward the goals it has defined, in the end, the greater consensus usually prevails.

An example of the power of the community to reach eventual agreement can be seen in the years of dialogue that preceded the trustees' decision in May 1987 to divest, excluding from the University's portfolios corporations doing business in South Africa, except those providing medical goods and humanitarian services, or those engaged in reporting the news. The divestiture vote validated the dedication of the Brandeis community to a cause that has captured the spirit and intellect of Brandeis students for decades.

Woodruff Hall became the first home of the Florence Heller Graduate School for Advanced Studies in Social Welfare, 1959. The former residence of the Middlesex University president served many functions for Brandeis before it was razed in 1969 to make way for the three new dormitory structures of the Rosenthal Quadrangle.

BELOW:
Dr. Charles I. Schottland, third president of Brandeis, ca. 1972. As Dr. Schottland has recalled, he left his "luxurious office in Washington" as United States Commissioner of Social Security to become the first Dean of the Florence Heller School for Advanced Studies in Social Welfare.

"I reported for work as the Dean of the Heller School on January 2, 1959. Our plan to open in September was looked upon as impractical since we had no faculty, no curriculum, no prospective students, no office or classroom space. I was urged to develop all of these resources and open the School in September 1960. This delay seemed to me unnecessary and I felt we could organize it by September 1959. And so we did – with a faculty of three, Robert Morris, David French, and myself. Our biggest surprise came when we sent out the announcement of the new school. We had counted on a response of twenty or twenty-five prospective students for the Ph.D. program, but we received more than 100 applications."

CHARLES I. SCHOTTLAND
Dean, Heller School, 1959–1970, 1976–1977
President, Brandeis University, 1970–1972

Completed in 1966, the present home of the Heller School was designed by Benjamin Thompson to fit its hillside site behind the Brandeis Libraries.

Philosopher Martin Buber during campus visit to deliver a Helmsley Dialogue Series lecture, March 28, 1957. Buber also met informally with faculty and students.

*For four decades Brandeis has
presented a diversity of political and
social points of view. Dorothy Day,
editor of the socialist* Catholic
Worker, *following her Gen Ed S
lecture in November 1958. Day
worked for the rights of the homeless
and in support of organized labor,
racial justice, and disarmament.*

Gen Ed S guest speaker Alger Hiss with Brandeis students, March 7, 1968. The famous Alger Hiss-Whittaker Chambers trials had made headlines in 1949 and 1950 and made a national figure of the former law clerk to Oliver Wendell Holmes.

"As a freshman from Texas in 1968, I especially remember the day when Martin Luther King, Jr. was killed and the manner in which the University responded. That evening, while meandering through the commons area of my dormitory, I came across an informal discussion group being conducted by my chemistry professor, Michael Henchman. I thought it strange that Professor Henchman would be leading such a session, for I had always thought of him strictly in terms of his masterful lectures in Chemistry 15A. It was then that I began to realize that his appearance in my dorm was no accident at all, but rather part of a carefully orchestrated response by the University to insure a faculty presence in each and every resident hall that evening, in order to help students as we searched for clues in understanding the implications of the events of that day. It was then that I began to appreciate the value of the total Brandeis experience and the multidimensional character of its faculty."

DAVID BELL '71

Dr. Martin Luther King, Jr. during his second campus visit, February 26, 1963. Dr. King returned to Brandeis to present a Helmsley Lecture Series talk on "Interracial Justice." In photograph to left facing Dr. King is Brandeis professor of politics and philosophy Herbert Marcuse.

*Children's Day sponsored by the
Waltham Group, December 10,
1967. As part of the annual Charity
Week activities, the Waltham Group
sponsored a day of fun for area
youngsters. More than 200 children
participated with nearly as many
Brandeis student escorts.*

Two participants at an Affirmative
Action seminar at the Heller School,
April 8, 1980.

Forty-six college-bound students and
thirty-two high school seniors from
all over the country attended the
federally-funded Upward Bound
Program at Brandeis, summer 1966.
Using a tutorial system, the program
was designed to improve students
skills and enhance opportunities for
future academic success. Students
spent half of each day working on
improving reading and writing
skills, the other half in courses that
provided an introduction to each of
the major divisions of the University
curriculum. The Upward Bound
Program at Brandeis continued for
more than a decade.

A 1964 mock presidential political convention at Brandeis took place in Shapiro Athletic Center.

148

"Brandeis has just celebrated its thirty-sixth consecutive commencement – a record that almost was aborted. I think I helped sustain that record. It was April 1970, a year in which the campus protests of the Vietnam War reached a peak. The seniors among the student activists decided that it would hardly be a fitting climax to their four years at Brandeis to have a normal commencement. The idea spread like wildfire: 'Let's cancel commencement!' A meeting was called to act on the idea. Some two hundred undergraduates crowded into the auditorium in Ford Hall. At the time I was a Brandeis graduate student. I had just completed my dissertation and was looking forward to receiving my Ph. D. I went to the meeting determined to cast my vote for holding a commencement. It soon became evident that this was likely to be a futile gesture. Not only was I the only graduate student present, but I was well into the age category that undergraduates characterized as 'not to be trusted.' Each student who spoke was more radical than the preceding one in advocating for 'No Commencement!' There was a near mob frenzy as the student chair yelled, 'Any final speaker before we vote?' With much trepidation I timidly raised my hand. A still set over the auditorium as I rose. Maybe my receding hairline and that I was wearing a tie caught their attention. With a quavering voice I told my story.

"'I agree with you guys that our government has been wrong in its policies in Vietnam and that commencement is a meaningless pageant. The only ones who would miss not having a commencement would be our families. For almost all of you that means your parents. For me that means my wife and my four young kids. It wasn't easy for them these past several years as I worked my tail off trying to finish my degree requirements. My kids have been busy making special signs they want to hold up when my name is called to get my degree. I wouldn't ask you guys to vote to have a commencement just for the sake of my wife and kids, but if any of you think it would mean something to your parents, you might consider the idea.' Someone then volunteered a compromise idea: commencement (grudgingly) but everyone wear red bands of protest. Motion passed (by a pretty good majority). And that was what happened at the nineteenth Brandeis commencement."

BERNARD REISMAN, PH.D. '70
Professor of American Jewish Communal Studies
Director, Hornstein Program in Jewish Communal Service

"*It was not easy to be affiliated with an institution of higher learning at the end of the sixties and early seventies. The problems were confronted not only by Morris Abram, Brandeis's second president, but by all college presidents nationwide. Those were years of unrest on every college campus, even the most venerable. Indeed, student revolt was an international phenomenon, from the barricaded streets of Paris to the strike-prone university in Mexico City.*"

RUTH G. ROSE
President, Brandeis University National Women's Committee, 1957–1960

The second president of Brandeis, Morris Abram, at a press conference following the January 8, 1969 takeover of Ford Hall. Abram's diary of the eleven-day occupation was later printed in The New York Times *Magazine.*

Future Massachusetts senator John Kerry was a member of the Vietnam Veterans Against the War when he addressed students in Schwartz Hall, September 26, 1971. Kerry's appearance was sponsored by Usdan Student Center and the University Pre-Law Society.

Brandeis students showing their
solidarity with the Brandeis
Afro-American Student
Organization in the takeover
of Ford Hall, January 8–18, 1969.

Georgia legislator Julian Bond
addressed a large campus gathering,
November 3, 1971. Other guest
speakers on the Brandeis campus
that same week were Kathleen
Cleaver and Dick Gregory.

Former Massachusetts governor Michael Dukakis, February 1980. Dukakis, who had lost his second gubernatorial campaign, spoke to a large campus gathering on behalf of the 1980 presidential campaign of Senator Edward Kennedy. Dukakis was then a teaching fellow at the Kennedy School of Government, Harvard University.

Then Massachusetts senator Paul Tsongas at a conference on his proposal for the establishment of a National Youth Service Program, February 2, 1980. Tsongas gave the keynote address and participated in seminars and discussion groups. Conference was cosponsored by the Brandeis Center for Public Service.

*The dedication of the Holocaust
Monument on the Brandeis campus,
April 1974. The monument was
erected in memory of victims of the
Holocaust and holds ashes from the
concentration camp at Treblinka.*

Anti-apartheid rally, April 1961.
Brandeis students picketed speech
by P. J. Nel, Director of the official
South African Information Service in
the United States. Anti-apartheid
petitions circulated the Brandeis
campus beginning in the mid-1950s.

Brandeis students constructed Shanty Town as a protest against apartheid and in support of the University's divesting of stock held in companies doing business in South Africa, February 1986. The Board of Trustees voted in favor of divestiture in May 1987.

President Evelyn Handler speaking to an anti-apartheid rally, 1986. In May 1987 the Brandeis Board of Trustees voted to divest of all holdings in South Africa except those providing medical goods or humanitarian services or involved in reporting the news.

BRANDEIS AT FORTY

"Meeting New Challenges"

"The years ahead will not be merely a replication of the past. If the early years of Brandeis can be likened to the growth and promise of childhood, the exuberance of adolescence, the drive and energy of young adulthood, then the years ahead will bring wisdom, and creativity, and the fulfillment of experience and maturity."

PRESIDENT EVELYN E. HANDLER
Inaugural Address, October 9, 1983

Forty years ago there was a sense of urgency and adventure at Brandeis, a spirit unwilling to accept limits, unwilling to be defined by the status quo. Sharing this pioneering spirit were scholars who came to teach at a fledgling university, students who risked educations at an unaccredited institution, and a foster family of supporters who gave of their time and resources long before there was an intimation that their hopes would be confirmed.

For some, the early exigencies of scarce funds, few buildings, and no alumni would have been viewed as insurmountable obstacles. But for the shapers of Brandeis these limitations were opportunities. As President Evelyn E. Handler remarked in her 1986 Founders' Day address, the courage that "built buildings where none had stood and programs where none had existed," will also forge the University's future with a new leadership and spirit dedicated to continuing a tradition of excellence.

Today Brandeis joins other American universities in the process of setting new priorities for the decades ahead. In a 1988 study by the Council for Advancement and Support of Education entitled "Higher Education and the Public Interest: A Report to the Campus," CASE executive director Gary H. Quehl provides an overview of the critical questions that will be faced by higher education in the next generation: "Periodically an issue of such magnitude arises that it galvanizes action throughout American society. Such issues over the past forty years have included dramatic advances in Soviet technology (Sputnik) and the civil rights and anti-Vietnam War movements. Today's omnibus issue is 'competitiveness,' the need to increase the country's economic productivity at home and abroad."

The period described by the CASE report is coincident with the history of Brandeis and the enumerated issues profoundly affected the University's development. Now the national concerns of career training and economic productivity are similarly resounding through the academy. As President Handler has observed, we are entering

OPPOSITE: *Students between classes on the steps of Rabb Graduate Center, 1987.*

President Evelyn E. Handler and Chairman of the Brandeis Board of Trustees Henry L. Foster, Commencement 1984. Dr. Foster was elected to the board in 1973 and served as its chairman from 1979 to 1985. Dr. Foster is a 1946 graduate of Middlesex Veterinary College and has been an active supporter of Brandeis for more than two decades. The construction of the Henry and Lois Foster Biomedical Research Laboratories in 1975 added an important new resource for biomedical research at the University.

a new era, a time when continual adaptation is the norm: "Today's discovery is tomorrow's relic. A university that does not move forward, falls behind."

But newness and change for their own sake have little validity for the University and a pledge to modernity does not betoken a rejection or betrayal of the institution's history and mission. Brandeis is poised once again to assume a leading role in developing new strategies for American education.

Despite the recent trend to establish institutions with more specialized, technical, and vocationally-oriented curricula, the challenge to the liberal arts is not new. For more than two decades specialization has been a pervasive force in academia, increasing each year as the world continues to grow more complex and more beholden to expanding technology. Brandeis has been at the forefront of efforts to guide liberal arts schools in devising ways to meet the educational needs of the future without abandoning a rich and time-honored tradition of American liberal arts education.

President Handler characterized the Brandeis criteria for incorporating new ideas into a traditional educational structure in a 1986 address at the University of Pittsburgh: "New fields of study should reflect conscious choices and a judgment as to their lasting value; they should not merely reflect a haste to follow the latest technological fad. When new fields of study are added to the curriculum, they are studied in the context of other studies, ensuring that Brandeis maintains historical, philosophical, and other perspectives on new knowledge."

Brandeis enters a new era with integrity and flexibility derived from a solid foundation established forty years ago by the University's shapers and nurtured by succeeding generations. To meet increasing demands for diversity, for example, the University has responded with interdisciplinary programs that enable students with particular interests to acquire the specialized knowledge they seek within the context of more broadly-based liberal arts majors. The range of programs available to undergraduate students in all concentrations includes curricula in Islamic and Middle Eastern Studies, Legal Studies, Peace Studies, Premedical Studies, Soviet Studies, and Women's Studies.

In recent years interdisciplinary intellectual discussion among Brandeis faculty developed into the Center for the Humanities, a forum for in-depth exploration of issues relevant to a variety of University disciplines. The Center now includes both a faculty seminar and a graduate student component, the latter is part of an interdisciplinary program in graduate education supported by a grant from the Mellon Foundation.

Brandeis has also taken advantage of natural and logical interrelations in the sciences. A concentration in engineering physics was recently developed as a vehicle for bringing applications into basic research. The engineering physics program emphasizes the fundamental scientific basis and application of physics in high technology and other areas, filling a recognized need now and in the future for engineer-scientists who understand both the theoretical and applied aspects of their discipline. The approach combines the fundamentals of physics with intensive experience in laboratories with modern equipment and instrumentation.

In 1983 a curriculum in computer science evolved from courses offered in the mathematics and physics departments. Built gradually and focussing first on theory, and in time, on applications, the Department of Computer Science in the Michtom School of Computer Science now includes both undergraduate and graduate programs of study.

The Department of Computer Science was one of the first to be approved by the Computing Sciences Accreditation Board in 1986. Although one of the University's newest departments, the program already has a record of significant contributions to the body of computer literature. Students have the opportunity to work closely with faculty in a time-honored tradition of undergraduate research at Brandeis. To date, computer science students have co-authored nearly twenty publications with department faculty members.

The computer science faculty is currently involved in pioneering work in the areas of parallel processing, logic programming, and data compression. Ongoing research with colleagues in other departments includes plans for establishing a new interdisciplinary research center that would encompass the University's expanding activities in computer science and artificial intelligence, cognitive science and perception, neuroscience, and structural biology.

Funding in the sciences has been a source of increasing concern to both academic administrators and researchers as essential facilities and equipment continue to develop at a dramatic pace while the cost of keeping current escalates. The infusion of energy and money into basic research during the 1950s was crucial to the early and rapid development of Brandeis. But the "golden age" of federal interest has long since receded and new sources of funding must be created and identified as the federal role in research continues

A computer room in the Feldberg Computer Center, 1985. The construction of the Feldberg Center in 1972 expanded teaching opportunities for both faculty and students and provided a campus-wide computer network.

to decline. A joint commitment to basic research was undertaken in 1988 by the Rosenstiel Center and the Markey Charitable Trust for the establishment of a new program in structural biology, a field in which the University pioneered research. The match with the Markey Foundation is an important paradigm for Brandeis in developing future relationships with private philanthropy in support of basic research as well as applications.

And in the social sciences, because of the rising concern with competitiveness and economic productivity, higher education is increasingly being asked to undertake research and instruction with an international perspective. Brandeis has begun to develop several approaches to research and education on a global scale.

The Lemberg Program in International Economics and Finance was inaugurated in 1986 to offer innovative graduate study for students planning careers in international business. Through a two-year master's program and a five-year B.A./M.A. option for qualified Brandeis undergraduates, the Lemberg Program provides a bridge between the disciplines and curricula offered by schools of business and international relations. Both American and foreign students are enrolled in the Lemberg Program which requires one semester of study at participating universities abroad. The program has already been cited for its innovative and imaginative use of the foreign study component.

To further enhance the development of Brandeis as an international educational and research institution, the Center for International and Comparative Studies was established in 1987 to facilitate faculty research, to foster intellectual interchange among faculty on campus, to enrich the educational life of both graduate and undergraduate students, and to provide administrative oversight and support for campus activities of an international and comparative nature in the social sciences.

In the creative arts as well, Brandeis has continued to seek ways of infusing new ideas and energy into a young, but established, program. In 1980, the music department became home to an accomplished young ensemble, the Lydian String Quartet. While large conservatories frequently offer students opportunities to work with an active professional performing group, it is rare for a liberal arts institution to afford students similar experiences. Research is not limited to the sciences and the notion of the artist-scholar has become an accepted tradition in all University disciplines. The highly-acclaimed Brandeis Quartet-in-Residence maintains an active presence on campus, coaching chamber music groups, conducting master classes, participating in lectures and demonstrations, and performing in concert series, frequently in important collaborations with faculty and student composers.

The Theatre Arts Program set a similar course in 1988 by launching the Brandeis Repertory Company, a fully professional Equity theatre ensemble based at the University. The BRC has been developed to assume a role in the growth of Boston as a theatre center. The BRC is in residence at the Spingold Theatre for a portion of each academic year, providing professional repertory theatre for Brandeis and community audiences while contributing to and benefitting from the energy of the graduate theatre program. By combining the artistry and professionalism of a repertory company with the ongoing activities of an academic theatre department faculty and student body, Brandeis seeks to fashion a new relationship between professional theatre and a research-oriented liberal arts institution.

But the times call for more than reworking older models or finding ways of incorporating new programs within more established ones. New matrices must be created if higher education is to continue to address emerging issues in an effective and responsible way. One solution for meeting both new challenges and new constraints, will be through multidisciplinary and multiuniversity programs, avoiding expensive duplications that do not efficiently make use of time, money, and resources, all at a premium in today's costly higher education market.

In 1987 the nation's first interdisciplinary, multiuniversity program for the study of public policy, the Gordon Public Policy Center, was established at Brandeis. The Gordon Center was designed to serve as a locus for shared research among experts in economics, political science, history, and law, fulfilling its mission through publications, seminars, and a wide range of research projects. At present, a dozen researchers from Brandeis and other area universities are based at the Gordon Center and many more participate in seminars and conferences related to government regulation, environmental policy, social policy, criminal justice, and public management.

The modern university is also involved in developing ways to bring together the resources of higher education with the needs of the wider community, which must look to an increasingly diversified base of public and private support for addressing a variety of social, economic, educational, and civic needs. In 1980 Brandeis set up the Humanities and the Professions Program in response to a request by the Commonwealth of Massachusetts. The Humanities and the Professions is a continuing education program in which great works of literature are used to help professionals explore some of the dilemmas they face daily in their professional lives. Among the groups involved in this successful experiment are judges and other law professionals, members of the medical and human service professions, as well as teachers and school administrators. Since its establishment, the

Humanities and the Professions has grown into a national endeavor reaching thousands of professionals in many fields.

Brandeis participates in many activities designed to benefit students from the region. In 1983 the University organized the Forefront Topics in Science series, a free Saturday campus lecture program for high school teachers and students. Devised to foster interest in the sciences, the lectures by members of the Brandeis School of Science faculty cover a variety of scientific fields. The Forefront Series involves students from high schools all over New England and the lectures are now being videotaped for wider accessibility by a national audience. The Creative Process Series is similar in design, presenting talks on creativity and the humanities for high school students and teachers. Lectures by Brandeis professors cover subjects ranging from an investigation of the vampire in social science to a discussion of the creative liar in American history and literature.

The Brandeis campus also sponsors summer programs. The "Summer Educational Adventure" comprises two sessions of study with courses that run the gamut from computer science to politics. The curriculum is designed to accommodate students with a variety of goals, including those engaged in a formal education program as well as those who want to sharpen professional skills or explore new interests.

In 1988 Brandeis was selected as a training site for the Minority Access to Research Careers Program (MARC) providing summer research experience for students from colleges and universities with large minority enrollments. MARC is funded by the National Institutes of Health and Brandeis joins such universities as Stanford, Columbia, and Cornell in teaming each MARC student with a faculty member in a campus research group to work on a special summer project. MARC students participate in research in biology, chemistry, biochemistry, psychology, and several interdisciplinary areas.

A new "Summer Discoveries Program" is currently being developed to offer a challenging residential experience to talented high school students selected nationwide. Courses in the Brandeis program will differ from those usually found in high school curricula and introductory college courses by offering an academic core primarily in science and elective courses in creative writing, politics, theatre, and architecture. Individual and group projects and laboratory and field experiences will be integral components as well as field trips and a variety of activities designed to enrich the students' educational and cultural experience.

After four decades of accomplishment, a young university can still look ahead to new milestones of achievement. In 1985 Brandeis was elected to the prestigious Association of American Universities as one of only fifty-six universities forming the national organization founded in 1900. Membership in the AAU is determined by appraisal of breadth and quality of graduate and professional work.

In 1987 Brandeis was invited to the newly-founded University Athletic Association, joining Emory University, the University of Chicago, Carnegie-Mellon University, New York University, Case Western Reserve University, Johns Hopkins University, Washington University, and the University of Rochester. For Brandeis it is the long-awaited opportunity to participate in a national competitive athletic program supportive of a broader academic mission.

And the Brandeis campus is still building for the future, undertaking a new construction effort to meet both current and anticipated University needs. Bulldozers are a

Members of the Brandeis University Board of Trustees, Founders' Day, 1986. Front row seated, left to right: Joseph M. Linsey, President Evelyn E. Handler, Chairman Leonard L. Farber, former Chairman Jacob Hiatt, Chancellor Emeritus Abram L. Sachar; second row seated, left to right: Secretary Stephen R. Reiner '61, Vice Chairman Stanley H. Feldberg, former Chairman Henry L. Foster, Vice Chairman Paul Levenson '52, Treasurer Maurice M. Cohen, Madeleine H. Russell; third row standing, left to right: former Chairman Norman S. Rabb, Faculty Representative Karen Klein, Myra Kraft '64, Student Representative Michele I. Masarsky '88, Student Representative Jacqueline Toribio, Barbara Miller, President, B.U.N.W.C.; back row standing, left to right: Faculty Representative George Ross, Student Representative Wayne Weitz '87, David F. Squire, Jeffrey H. Golland '61, President, Alumni Association, Walter A. Rosenblith, Robert Shapiro '52, Malcolm L. Sherman, Rena J. Blumberg '56, Gustav Ranis '52, Esther Kartiganer '59, and Arnold Cutler. Chairman Farber's tribute to the Board: "Among the unsung heroes at Brandeis are the members of the Board of Trustees who selflessly give so much of their time and energy in an endeavor to help achieve the University's mission of excellence. Their sole compensation is the satisfaction of seeing Brandeis hold its place of distinction among the most respected of academic institutions."

common sight as they were in the early days, when they came to "a campus stern and rockbound, appropriate to the carving out of a new institution," as Rachel Mellinger observed in an article on Brandeis in the October 1955 issue of *Mademoiselle* magazine.

In 1983 the new Farber Library was dedicated, increasing the collection of the Brandeis University Libraries to well over one million books and microfiche. The completion of the Ziv Quadrangle in 1987 provided additional dormitory rooms as well as a multipurpose commons structure for a variety of campus uses. The renovation and expansion of the Sherman Student Center has increased dining services, furnished additional student activities areas, and given Brandeis a new conference facility to serve the needs of both on campus and off campus groups.

Further proposed construction includes a new athletic-convocation center enabling Brandeis to evolve into a major collegiate athletic locus, hosting national tournaments in track, volleyball, softball, swimming, and tennis. The proposed new center will be built adjacent to the Shapiro Athletic Center and the Linsey Sports Center and will include a field house large enough to accommodate convocations and special events.

Four members of the Class of '53 reminiscing at their thirty-fifth reunion, June 1988. The Brandeis Alumni Association was founded in 1952 and now includes more than 20,000 alumni with eleven chartered chapters throughout the United States.

The completion of the Ziv Quadrangle in the fall of 1987 provided new dormitory space for a largely resident undergraduate student body. The Ziv dorms are adjacent to the first new dormitories constructed on the campus, the Ridgewood Quadrangle, completed in 1950.

Brandeis will continue to face important new challenges as it seeks to meet the needs of the next century while sustaining those qualities that have enabled it to remain a coherent institution for four decades. In November 1986 the University celebrated its first Founders' Day, a tribute, as President Handler noted, "to the people who created it and those whose support has enabled us to continue to aspire and to grow." The commemoration of the first Founders' Day included dedication of specially-commissioned portraits of the University's presidents, in recognition of their contributions to the growth and development of Brandeis.

And the founding spirit was still in evidence as the University announced the launching of its first nationally-organized volunteer fund-raising effort. The goal of the five-year Campaign for Brandeis is to raise $200 million for a multitude of critical needs, including support of faculty excellence and achievement; broadening of opportunities to a more diverse student body; improvement and expansion of facilities and support services; and the establishment of new programs to enable the University to continue responding to the needs of modern society with new and revised academic models.

President Handler acknowledged the singular mission of the University and the Brandeis community at this first Founders' Day celebration: "All institutions about which we care deeply have a special ethos, a special character, a special vision of themselves and their future." Yet the distinction of an institution rests not only on what it has achieved, but also on what it has the capacity and the will to accomplish in the future. The founders of Brandeis, and those who have nurtured the University since, endeavored to build an institution that would not only aspire to and attain excellence, but also move beyond the fulfillment of the early promise to even greater accomplishment.

At forty, Brandeis continues to turn for support to generations of foster alumni whose enthusiasm and dedication provide the vision and inspiration, and to the University alumni who have come of age to join in forging the University's future.

Once again the Brandeis community is poised for new challenges. The energies of the board of trustees, fellows, alumni, and Women's Committee have been rededicated to meeting the goals that have been set to ensure the University's continued growth and development and commitment to excellence. Brandeis at forty approaches the future with the same creativity and sense of adventure that have characterized this extraordinary institution from the beginning.

"If we reflect on the state of mind of the community that founded Brandeis, of the faculty members who responded to the invitation to teach at a small and unknown school, and the students of the early years who risked coming to an unaccredited university, we see a common characteristic. They shared a pioneering spirit and a creative energy unwilling to accept limits, unwilling to accept that some things just couldn't be done. In undertaking a new adventure, in allowing imagination to flow, in taking risks, they found a special excitement that has come to be known as the Brandeis spirit. . . .

"All institutions about which we care deeply have a special ethos, a special character, a special vision of themselves and their future. Brandeis is no different. For Brandeis, the vision is an educational institution grounded in the rich cultural heritage of a people. A heritage that puts the highest values on education, on wisdom, on knowledge, on love of learning, on the search for truth, and on service to others.

"But that vision and tradition speak to all people – not just to those who founded and sustained Brandeis. The gift of Brandeis and of a Brandeis education is a gift to the whole of American society, indeed, to the world. . . .

"And it is precisely because we have a vision – a vision of what we have been, a vision of what we are, and a vision of what we can become – that we know we can succeed. In fewer than four decades, we have attained that which once appeared unattainable. Our faculty continues to be ever more creative. Our students continue to seek the challenge of exploring new educational frontiers. Our alumni continue to grow and have taken up the obligation to give back to this institution something of the value that Brandeis gave to them.

"Our pioneering work of today will shape the Brandeis of tomorrow, the Brandeis that will educate the leaders of the twenty-first century. . . . In many ways, we have only just embarked on a great educational adventure."

PRESIDENT EVELYN E. HANDLER
Founders' Day Convocation, November 2, 1986

The presidents of Brandeis
University at the first Founders' Day
Celebration, October 1986. From
left, Marver H. Bernstein,
1972–1983; Charles I. Schottland,
1970–1972; Evelyn E. Handler,
1983–; Morris B. Abram, 1968–1970;
and Abram L. Sachar, 1948–1968.

From left, professor Lawrence
Kirsch, associate professor Craig
Blocker, and associate professor
James R. Bensinger in the Fermi
Physics Lab at Brandeis, ca. 1985.
The Brandeis laboratory is part of
the renowned Illinois Fermi National
Accelerator Laboratory (Fermilab)
and links the work of Brandeis
physicists with that of other
scientists around the world.

Portrait of jazz musician Ricky Ford
at the ninth annual Louis Armstrong
Jazz Concert, 1987. Funds from the
concert help sustain the Louis
Armstrong Scholarship Fund at
Brandeis, established in 1979 to
found and support the Brandeis Jazz
Ensemble.

A student at work in the
Goldman-Schwartz Art Studios,
December 1987.

Amherst vs. Brandeis in the 1987
homecoming soccer match.

Senator Paul Simon addressed the Brandeis Forum as a 1988 Democratic Party hopeful, October 1987. The 1987-1988 Forum also sponsored visits by Richard Gephardt, Albert Gore, Pierre DuPont, and Jack Kemp.

"I first set foot on the Brandeis campus in the spring of 1951 when I arrived for an interview. President Sachar led me to his office in Woodruff Hall, a small white frame house that served for all administrative functions. He bounded up the steps, opened the screen door, and suddenly swung around, making an expansive gesture with his arm in the direction of the campus, and exclaimed, 'Harvard started with only ten acres; already we have two hundred.' That was my first introduction to the Brandeis fever, the burning conviction that within a generation we would establish a small university of excellence. That was a conviction that burned within us. We believed in the idea of Brandeis, in President Sachar, in ourselves. We were passionately committed to the school. It was ours. It wasn't just a place where we had jobs. It was part of our lives, part of family. We loved it, we knew we could shape it, and we worked with a furious intensity for it. We turned our deficiencies into assets. Because we were so small, we were forced to cultivate interdisciplinary approaches to teaching and learning, and we boasted about that. We had four schools, but no departments, no walls between disciplines. Every member of the faculty was supposed to be able to cover at least two traditional disciplines (mine were history and politics). As a young instructor, I had four different courses. I met each class three times a week. Once, George Alpert, the chairman of the board of trustees, asked me how much I taught. I replied, 'Twelve hours.' He thought a moment and said, 'That's a pretty good working day. President Sachar sure expects a lot from his faculty.' He sure did, and he got it. Our salaries were pretty low, but we got a great deal of psychic income in return. When I saw the campus in October 1987 for the first time in seventeen years, I felt pride and exaltation: the devotion, the sacrifices, and the commitment had all been worthwhile."

LEONARD W. LEVY
Warren Professor of American Constitutional Studies, 1951–1970

*A seminar in the Sachar Center
conducted by assistant professor of
economics Gary Jefferson, 1987.*

A view of the Brandeis libraries,
ca. 1985. The Goldfarb and Farber
libraries and Rapaporte Treasure
Hall symbolize four decades of
dedication by the Brandeis
University National Women's
Committee and the generosity
of the Brandeis foster family.

Members of the Brandeis plant
maintenance staff in a relaxing
moment at the annual staff picnic,
June 1987.

Students in front of the Rose Art Museum at dusk, ca. 1985. The sculpture "Neon for the Rose Art Museum" by artist-in-residence Stephen Antonakos, was commissioned by the Rose Purchase Fund and featured in the ninth Patrons and Friends of the Rose exhibition, Stephen Antonakos: Neons and Drawings.

The first residents of the new Ziv Quadrangle on moving day, September 1987.

The front of the Rosenstiel Center for Basic Medical Sciences Research is graced by the eighteen-foot "Wand of Inquiry" by Lila Katzen, 1986. The two-part sculpture was commissioned by the Rosenstiel Foundation and installed in September 1983.

A 1986 view of Mailman House, the University's Psychological Counseling Center as well as home to psychology department laboratories and seminar rooms. Mailman House, designed in 1972 by Harrison and Abramovitz, is sited next to the Stoneman Infirmary in the shadow of the Castle.

OPPOSITE:
The reflecting pool and Berlin Chapel, spring 1984. The Chapel Field Area was designed by Harrison and Abramovitz to ensure the tranquility and serenity of this corner of the Brandeis campus.

A view of the new Sherman Dining Facility under construction looking up the hill to the Science Quadrangle and the buildings of Rosenstiel and Foster, fall 1987.

"We who came in 1948 'didn't we think it was mighty great' – or so the song goes. The truth is that we, the class of '52, were a mixture of ordinary pick-ups, extraordinary risk takers, and innocents, not fully aware of the size of the gamble we were taking in opting for an unaccredited institution. Brandeis was truly built 'on a blueprint and a prayer' – we didn't even have one wing – and, as we sloshed through the mud between the Castle and Science Hall, some of us began to wonder increasingly about the blueprint and to rely more and more on prayer. Nevertheless, in our heart of hearts, we always knew – knew that we were safe, that American Jewry would never permit their one gift to nonsectarian higher education in this country to fail – not even to flounder. Thus when accreditation came, and Phi Beta Kappa, and graduate school acceptance rates – and all the rest – at unheard of, record, speed – we didn't quite understand what the fuss was all about: after all, we had known it all along.

"And now, forty years later, what are our thoughts? Undoubtedly those were extraordinarily 'special' pioneering days – imagine being a senior for four years! – and they will indeed never come back, nor should we want them to. There is only one creation and there is no point in trying to turn back the clock. Does that mean that the excitement has necessarily gone out of the place? Emphatically not. What we feel today is a different kind of exhilaration, one that comes with mature middle age, one that is built on consolidation and enrichment instead of take-offs and gambles. A Brandeis 'first' celebrating our fortieth anniversary may seem pale by comparison with the other milestones we all remember so well – but it really isn't. The kind of commitment and support required now – within an external climate which is much more difficult than in those days – is in a sense more nuanced and more precious than the enthusiasms of childhood and adolescence. The challenge now is not to abandon the search for excellence and not to 'settle' for survival. There is plenty of pioneering that remains to be done. It means putting our energies into securing Brandeis's special place – outrageously quickly achieved – among the quality institutions of this country. It means refusing to be sidetracked by differences on tactics and personalities. It means – once again – ignoring the mud at our feet and lifting our eyes to the exciting challenges that lie ahead."

GUSTAV RANIS '52
Secretary, Board of Trustees

Renovation and new construction of the Sherman Dining Hall facility, fall 1987.

PAGES 182–183:
A bird's-eye view of students at work in Farber Library, ca. 1986.

PAGES 184–185:
The campus still serves as classroom, ca. 1985.

PAGE 186:
A serene corner of the Brandeis campus near the Sachar International Center, fall 1987.

CLOSING ENDLEAVES:
Panorama of Brandeis University Commencement.